Thirty-Life Crisis

D0967672

Thirty-Life Crisis

Navigating My Thirties,
One Drunk Baby Shower
at a Time

Lisa Schwartz

GRAND CENTRAL
PUBLISHING

NEW YORK   BOSTON

Some names and identifying details have been changed.

Copyright © 2019 by Lisa Schwartz

Cover design by Liz Casal. Cover photograph © Joanna Degeneres.
Cover copyright © 2019 by Hachette Book Group, Inc.

Hachette Book Group supports the right to free expression and the value of copyright.
The purpose of copyright is to encourage writers and artists to produce the creative
works that enrich our culture.

The scanning, uploading, and distribution of this book without permission is a theft of
the author's intellectual property. If you would like permission to use material from the
book (other than for review purposes), please contact permissions@hbgusa.com. Thank
you for your support of the author's rights.

Grand Central Publishing
Hachette Book Group
1290 Avenue of the Americas, New York, NY 10104
grandcentralpublishing.com
twitter.com/grandcentralpub

First Edition: August 2019

Grand Central Publishing is a division of Hachette Book Group, Inc. The Grand
Central Publishing name and logo is a trademark of Hachette Book Group, Inc.

The publisher is not responsible for websites (or their content) that are not owned by the
publisher.

The Hachette Speakers Bureau provides a wide range of authors for speaking events.
To find out more, go to www.hachettespeakersbureau.com or call (866) 376-6591.

Library of Congress CIP data has been applied for.

ISBNs: 978-1-5387-6309-4 (paperback), 978-1-5387-6310-0 (ebook)

Printed in the United States of America

LSC-C

10 9 8 7 6 5 4 3 2 1

*To my mom and dad, who told me
I could do anything, not thinking
I'd write a book. I love you.*

Contents

Contents

Thirty-Life Crisis

The Author of This Book Took My Virginity: A Foreword by Shane Dawson

It was a hot summer's night in the magical city of Hollywood and an even *hotter* summer's night in the one-bedroom apartment of struggling actress Lisa Schwartz. This wasn't because the people inside were having heated, passionate sex, but because Lisa didn't want to pay for air-conditioning and would rather occasionally put her head in the freezer and her tits in the fridge. I watched her do this one night as I sat bottomless on the couch with a large ice cube wedged in at the top of my hairy ass crack. As I adjusted the towel underneath me to make sure I wasn't getting ice-poop-sweat drips on her couch, I thought to myself, *Tonight's the night. I'm going to lose my virginity!*

Me: "Lisa? Are you almost numb in there?"
Lisa: "Yeah! I'm just gonna grab a cold bottle of Tito's to straddle. You want anything?"

Drip.

Me: "Maybe some more ice."

Drip. Drip.

Me: "And another towel. Something earth toned."

Lisa sat down next to me with the hardest nipples I had ever seen. Even harder than mine when I found out TLC was rebooting *Trading Spaces* with all the original designers coming back! Neighbors switching houses and letting each other redecorate their living rooms?! Talk about drama with some "roomspiration" on the side! I'm PINTERESTed! You're probably thinking that's something a straight guy wouldn't watch…and you would be right. But no spoilers—I'll let Lisa tell you more about that later in this book. Back to the hot summer's night of 2012.

Me: "When do you think you'll get
     air-conditioning?"
Lisa: "When that thinner, younger version of me
     stops booking every fuckin' commercial on TV."
Me: "Who?"
Lisa: "Her name's Amy. I saw it on the sign-in sheet.
     I hope she gets fat from all those yogurt com-
     mercials she books."

She shoved the cold bottle of Tito's in between her legs and let out a grunt.

Lisa: "I need to book something soon. The number
in my bank account's getting scarily close to
the number on my scale, and I like to keep
those far away from each other."
Me: "You could always gain a thousand pounds!"

She stared at me unamused. I dripped.

Lisa: "I wonder if they'll bring back those Dove com-
mercials where they have all the big ladies talk
about how much they love their creases. I could
pretend to love my creases too if I got residuals."

As Lisa rotated the thawed part of the Tito's bottle
away from her now purple vagina, I looked into her eyes
and saw something she always seemed to have lingering
in there: uncertainty. She was constantly battling voices
inside her head that were screaming that she wasn't good
enough, pretty enough, thin enough, talented enough, or,
most importantly, successful enough. It was something
that would send me into a whirlwind of confusion because
I didn't understand how somebody so beautiful, so talented, so hilarious, and, most importantly, *so good* could be
so hard on themselves.

The first time I saw Lisa was a few years prior, and I
thought she was the prettiest girl I had ever seen in my
entire nineteen years of life. We were total strangers,

sitting across from each other in a seedy audition room in the slums of Hollywood. As she stared at her script, I stared at her face and couldn't stop thinking about how lucky she was to be so fucking beautiful. I thought about how all the other girls in the room were probably looking at her with spite and how the guy with the six-pack sitting next to me was probably going to be making out with her on set later, after they both inevitably got the job because, why wouldn't they? Now as I look back, I realize while I was thinking about how perfect she was, she was thinking about all the things she wished she could change about herself. Even to this day she doesn't realize how incredible she really is. But once again, no spoilers. I'm sure she will give you lots of insight into what goes on inside her head later.

Me: "Should we…go to the bedroom?"
Lisa: "I'm too hot to dry hump. Can we do it after my sweat crystalizes?"
Me: "Well…I was thinking…maybe…"
Lisa: "What?"

DRIP.

Me: "Maybe we could try…to…"

My heart started to race and I felt like I was going to pass out more than I already had in this $1,200-a-month walk-in oven.

Me: "Not…dry hump…"

Lisa slowly ripped the Tito's from her inner thighs like a child's tongue off a frozen street pole. She placed it on the coffee table and took a deep breath.

Lisa: "You sure you're ready?"

(Quick backstory: I always said I wanted to wait till marriage to have sex for religious reasons. The truth was that I was nervous about my oddly large balls and my penis's resting state. I don't want to go into detail, but it kind of looks like a feeder mouse. Don't worry—when it's hard, it's perfectly slightly below average and weirdly red.)

Me: "Well…I was thinking…I wanted to wait to
        have sex with the person I knew I was going to
        spend the rest of my life with…and I know I
        want to spend it with you."

The uncertainty that was usually always somewhere in her eyes disappeared. We had only been dating for a few months, but the connection we had was so strong that we both knew it was going to last forever. A tear rolled down her cheek and then one rolled down mine. I was more sure that I wanted my first time to be with her than I've ever been sure of anything in my life.

Now, I'm not going to get graphic and tell you about how the sex was, but I will tell you this: Her room was ten degrees hotter than the rest of her apartment, so my ass sweat soaked through all her bed sheets and caused her mattress to mold. I know, a true love story. There's nothing more romantic than having your girlfriend ask if you peed the bed or if it was just a puddle from your back fat and ass sweat. You know, just like in all the good romance movies.

When we realized that night that we were going to be together for the rest of our lives, we weren't wrong. We might not sweat naked together in a humid apartment in Hollywood anymore, but I still consider Lisa my family. My first love, my first time, my first real relationship, my first partner in crime, and now my first book foreword.

The reason I decided to tell you this story wasn't because I wanted to brag about having sex with the author of this book or to give you vivid details about the shape and general vibe of my penis. It's because I waited twenty-three years to make love to someone who I didn't think existed. Someone who would make me feel comfortable enough to take off my clothes for the first time even though I hated my body. Someone who I trusted enough to share so much of myself and so much of my life with. Someone who could make me laugh harder than anyone I know and cry with me when I didn't know who I was. Someone who I could talk to for hours and not be constantly thinking about my next meal. Someone who said they didn't mind my big balls because they were *"big just like my heart."*

Foreword

This book isn't just written by a funny woman with stories to tell. This book is written by a woman whose stories are worth telling. I'm so proud to introduce this book to you, written by a woman who is hilarious, dark, wise, insightful, and has always been good enough: Lisa Schwartz.

Introduction

Raised on Seinfeld

> *You know, if you take everything I've accomplished in my entire life and condense it down into one day, it looks decent.*
>
> —George Costanza

Entering your thirties SUCKS. Ok, that was dramatic. Not EVERYTHING about it sucks. You're finally in charge of your own life and can do all the things your parents told you not to do, like have popcorn and wine for dinner, or stay up for hours watching shitty reality TV shows while ordering useless products on Amazon Prime. (I was desperate to try an LED rainbow showerhead precisely because my parents refused to buy me one when I was younger. As it turns out, they were right for saying no. It was a complete waste of money, and now I shower underneath a dull, red flashing light.)

As entertaining as these snack-induced comas, *Bachelor* binges, and tipsy online purchases can be, hitting your thirties is far tougher than any guilty pleasure or useless purchase can mend. The minute you turn thirty, everything starts to change. The bills on your desk get higher, your metabolism gets slower, and your friends get married and have babies. Now, don't get me wrong—I love my friends. I want the best for them, including a wedding with an open bar and little humans I can give back when they start to cry. However, these sudden surges of change sent my brain into a marathon of questioning. If they are settling down and having kids, am I supposed to? Do I want to? If I do, do I have to do it *now*? I was just about to finally start *Game of Thrones*!

This thought cycle usually leads to a period of binge drinking and sleeping with random dudes as a "fuck you" to living life the "right way," followed by a sob session with a therapist who I'm certain counts the minutes till we're done, topped off by a plate of fries with a side of "I should try to be like everybody else. Right?" Shit, I'm exhausted and we've only just begun. Welcome to your thirties.

There are plenty of books out there to help see you through your "quarter-life crisis"—see *Chicken Soup for Your 25-Year-Old Soul Who Is Still Living Off Top Ramen and Trying to Figure Out Which Minimum-Wage Job to Stick Out*, aka *The Holy Bible for Student Loan Victims and Soon-to-Be Struggling Artists*—but no one warns you about the *thirty-life crisis*, when the microwaved noodles and cater waiter jobs of your twenties start to feel like a quaint walk in the park and when the proverbial umbilical cord to a noncommittal life of partying and dreaming gets cut off by wedding invites and 401(k)s. Sadly, the dream boards made with the assistance of that epic joint are thrown into the trashcan as your friends succumb to the once proclaimed enemy, "the man." Not to mention the "where are we going to eat" conversations turn into "where is this going" in the blink of an eye. In just one decade, inquiring about your relationship status shifts from being perceived as clingy and even crazy because you have "so much time" ahead of you to being the norm and even a societal expectation because you're "running out of time," you old hag. Holy hell, where is the book for that?

Don't freak out—I promise it gets better. If you've ever experienced the feeling of your age wearing you down, or have felt like you were on a different path than the people around you, I got your back. It took me thirty-five years to accept the fact that I can't do life like everyone else, even if it would be easier for me to just climb the corporate ladder, settle down, and pop out a kid or two. Every other moron is capable of doing it; why can't I? The answer: *Seinfeld*.

Seriously. Every Thursday night, my family and I turned our dining room chairs toward the TV and watched *Seinfeld* intently. It didn't occur to me until just now that I was far more influenced by this show than I ever realized. Think about it. The four main characters were single, independent misfits in their thirties. They lived alone, overthought everything, and made love look tedious. *Seinfeld* laid my life out before me—I just didn't know it yet.

One time someone told me I reminded them of George Costanza. At first, I was totally insulted. I look way better posing in my underwear on a couch. But then I realized they were right. I'm a tiny neurotic Jew with a knack for doing things the wrong way, and I have been known on several occasions to dig a dessert out of the trashcan.

Of course, a TV show can't be the only explanation for an aversion to the norm. Personally, I like to blame my parents. (That's what they're there for, right?) The reality is mine are actually delightful humans. But they are just that—human. Without knowing it, their innate fears and overt neuroses rubbed off on me at a very young age. For example, thanks to them, I will NEVER check my bags at the airport curb, I will ALWAYS have an "out" for every social event, and I will NEVER be fully comfortable in large crowds. I'm a real good time. On top of all that, my parents' divorce inadvertently hindered my shot at ever trusting in true love. Because I saw firsthand that a beautiful couple, with a good family, steady incomes, and great senses of humor, were capable of falling out of love, I was left incapable of believing in eternal love. At least my skepticism justifies my three-dates-and-quit rule.

I know I sound like a millennial (if only I still looked like one), complaining and blaming everyone else. I am. But I also take full responsibility for my relentless desire to overanalyze life, all for the sake of figuring out what the fuck we are expected to be doing here. The impetus of my thirty-life crisis.

Through my various awkward experiences, which I'm probably going to regret sharing, I hope that I can give comfort to those going through this less-documented rite of passage. The neurotic ones trying to take the unconventional path while still questioning themselves along the way. The ones who have had to parent a parent, unprepared, as they lay sobbing in your arms. The ones who have finally accepted they need help because leaving the house has become increasingly more difficult. The ones who relate to being called crazy on a first date, or who have had to explain to a grandparent, time and again, why they're still single. The ones who talk to their pets, dance to the music playing in their heads, and can't wait to get home to rip off their Spanx. And especially to the ones who are exhausted by the tears and are desperate for the giggles. In the end, the only way to deal with the toughest shit life throws at you is to laugh.

Even though my thirties have been one hell of an emotional roller coaster, at least I can share with you what I've learned so far and chalk my many failures up to research. You're welcome. Also, thank you. My breakdowns now have a purpose.

Finally, a warning: This book will be unfiltered and often unladylike. It has to be; it's real. It's funny at times, sad at others, and humiliating, to say the least. I'm not holding back, because humans need to know that other humans are just as fucked up as they are, and that's ok. In fact, sometimes it's downright awesome. After all, why do you think *Seinfeld* is still so popular? I'll always find solace in George Costanza. For I am Lisa Schwartz, "Lord of the Idiots." Let's do this.

Gender-Reveal Party—Yes, It's a Fucking Thing

You gotta see the baby!
> —Jerry Seinfeld as every annoying
> baby-crazed person

Change is hard. I've never been good at it, no matter how many pillows with inspirational quotes I buy. Intellectually, I know that change is inevitable and usually leads to the next awesome chapter in your life. Yet, even knowing this, any shift in my routine throws me for a huge emotional loop.

Growing up, all I wanted was a dog. I would beg my parents, daily, to let us have one. After a couple of years of incessant begging, I decided to take matters into my own hands. I was ten at this point, and being in double digits meant getting shit done. I did extensive research on the breed I wanted and made a list of all the things I would personally do to help take care of it. Funny how that list magically disappeared when the dog arrived. Nevertheless, my parents fell for my master plan. To seal the deal, I had found an ad in the *PennySaver* for a litter of the cutest miniature schnauzers. For the record, I endorse rescuing dogs, but at that time that wasn't as common. Plus, we're Jewish and allergic to everything, so finding a hypoallergenic dog was a box on the list I needed to check to ensure victory. It worked! Within hours, we were in the car, headed down to the middle of nowhere to meet the puppy of my dreams. Everything was going just as I had planned.

We had tickets to see a play on the night we finally brought the puppy home. Being the Schwartzes, we weren't going to waste money and not attend. So, we set the pup up in his new crate and headed out. In the car, I started to cry. Then, I panicked. Before I knew it, I was basically hyperventilating. It wasn't that I was upset we had left the puppy at home; instead I was having a full-blown anxiety attack over the fact that we got the dog in the first place.

"What if everything changes? What if everything is different? What if it was a bad idea? What if…what if…?" I shouted with boogers and tears sprinting down my face.

I honestly don't remember my parents' response. I was too worked up to listen, with my brain was going a million miles a minute. It was totally absurd because I wanted the dog so badly, but once I got him, I freaked out and immediately thought we should give him back. That, my friends, is what my OCD looks like (diagnosed, unfortunately not a hyperbole). A spiral of thoughts, loss of emotional control, full-blown panic, a complete aversion to change.

I ended up loving that dog. Max Farfel Schwartz. A

gray miniature schnauzer with a terrible disposition and giant balls. Guessing the former had something to do with the latter. Max was my best friend and a huge part of my teenage life. He died when I was in college. Apparently, he went blind and kept walking into the pool. There was always a cover on, though, so he never fell in. He just stood there in terror, like Jesus walking on water, but the neurotic version. Eventually my parents had to put him down. Shortly afterward, they had to put down their marriage too. I don't think the former had anything to do with the latter, but I'd have to ask. All these years later, my brother and I still sign Max's name on cards. Always accompanied by a little paw print and an "RIP." I'm not sure if we do it as a joke or as a serious *in memoriam*. Probably both.

I use this story a lot when trying to explain my reactions to change. Most people are able to go with the flow, or at least try to. To see someone, like me, freak out over the smallest and often most unexciting things is hard for many to understand. As absurd as the dog story is, it paints a picture of how I operate.

When I turned thirty, change started coming faster and more often. With that, my panic attacks came stronger and lasted longer. It wasn't that I was upset that I was getting older; I was upset that everything was shifting. My friends were getting married and having babies, and the dynamics of the friendships were evolving. It was all freaking me the fuck out.

Randi, Jessica, and I had been friends since we were in middle school. We met doing children's theater and spent our summers having slumber parties and rehearsing our jazz squares. We stayed loosely in touch during high school and college, and then reunited once we all moved back to Los Angeles. When we did, it was like we had never left. In fact, our bond became even stronger. Ever since then we have been like the Three Amigos, Charlie's Angels, the Powerpuff Girls, or some other cute trio reference.

I've always done better in a group of three. Growing up it was Caitlin, Kit, and me. Now Randi, Jess, and me. I think there is some sort of buffer with three. One-on-one, you have no choice but to reveal everything about yourself. With three, sometimes you can go a whole hangout without ever really focusing on you. It's a nice escape from the antagonistic self-analysis I do on a daily basis.

The three of us spend copious amounts of time together. We travel together, laugh together, cry together, and eat unhealthy amounts of French fries together. We're like the cast of *Now and Then*. Except there are only three of us, and I call dibs on not being Rosie O'Donnell. These ladies are my heart, my soul, and my one constant amongst all the change.

Randi is a preschool administrator, and a very good one at that. She is tremendously patient, humbly brilliant, and she has a heart of gold. I don't exactly know what that means, but it seems appropriate. She is subtle and thoughtful, but give her a glass of wine and the performer in her arrives. With Randi, I am comforted by our parallel anxieties and our need to please others. I can confide in her when I'm feeling overwhelmed or upset. Most of the time, we just have a silent understanding that we are on the same page. We appreciate the art of shopping, decorating, and hermitting. We have an ongoing battle over who uses WebMD the most. Now we have a secret book club, mostly because we don't want to deal with other people. Randi, this book better be next month's pick.

Jessica is like no one I have ever met before. She enters a room, and everyone knows she's there. She's eccentric and hysterical. Crazy but stable. She is the life of the party but half the time would prefer to be home in her sweatpants, cutting her cuticles obsessively. When I'm with her, I don't have to worry about holding a conversation, or keeping things interesting. She takes me out of my comfort zone and gives me permission to let loose. A good time is built in anytime Jess is around. What I really love about Jessica is what's underneath all that. She's authentic and unapologetic. She's the least judgmental person I know. She's constantly just trying to figure out what we are all doing here and why. Also, whether or not a parallel universe exists, which we've spent hours on the couch talking about. Our conclusion: abso-fucking-lutely.

I feel like I land somewhere in between the two of them. I think on the outside I'm more of a Jessica, but inside I'm a Randi. When I'm with both of them, though, I finally feel like myself. For a socially anxious oddball, this is the greatest gift I could ever receive. These women have made me the woman I am today, and I am beyond grateful for our friendship. Except for when Jessica doesn't have coffee in the morning. It's not pretty, and I don't want any part of it.

When we entered our thirties, we started to collectively feel the changes around us. With every baby shower invite, we held on to each other a little tighter. We also started drinking a little heavier. As our friends started getting pregnant and our social circle starting changing, we noticed we were no longer the center of the party. In fact, we were the annoying girls that needed to put down the champagne and invest in a cardigan set. We knew it, but we weren't about to do it. Instead, we would sit in the back of the room at every baby shower and roll our eyes as we pounded the drinks we'd snuck in. We weren't ready.

No matter how much we wanted to slow everything down, these ridiculous events were being thrown at us left and right. We had no choice—we had to suck it up, put on our floral-print dresses, and show up with some bullshit gift we got off some bullshit registry. Which, by the way, I don't think is very fair. You had an engagement party, a bridal shower, a bachelorette weekend, and a fucking wedding. Now you're having two baby showers, a baby naming, and then a birthday for every year that kid is alive. What next? Am I going to have to celebrate your vagina snapping back into place after you push that third child out? FUCK YOU. I'm broke, with an unjustifiably loose vagina, and I haven't received a real gift since my fucking Bat Mitzvah, where I mostly received weird coins that are still sitting, dusty, in some cabinet at my dad's house. You know what? I'm going to get me a registry and make you buy *me* shit if you keep inviting me to these ridiculous parties where all you serve is iced tea and little sandwiches. Give me a full-size sandwich and a glass of wine or I will go insane.

Which, I admittedly did more often than I'd like to admit (but do in this book). I would like to point out that this time was absolutely valid. This time exceeded all the other times, and then some. This time pushed the celebration limits to such an extreme that I nearly lost my mind. I certainly lost my pride.

It was a perfect summer day. The kind of day you want to spend drinking with your two best friends by the pool, laughing about the shitty date you went on last night with the guy who dropped the "I live on my ex-girlfriend's couch" bomb, and planning the next time the three of you can ditch town and drink your body weight in wine. Oh, glorious summer—the sun was bright, the energy was electric, and the three of us…were stuck going to a gender-reveal party. Yes, insert that record scratch. I did, in fact, say GENDER-REVEAL PARTY. As if the two baby showers we had attended for this fetus wasn't enough, we had to pretend to care whether it was coming out with a penis or a vagina. Let me tell you, there are very few things I actually care about. Teeny-tiny private parts are certainly not one of them.

In recent years, I have come to realize the power of saying no. If I don't want to do something, I don't have to. I'm an adult and I owe that decision to myself. The power of no is a strong and an empowering thing. The power of obligation and guilt due to years of friendship, however, is stronger. So, we pulled ourselves together and went to the damn party.

We were supposed to dress in the color that represented the sex we thought the baby would come out as. Really, we all just wanted to wear black, but Randi wore pink, I wore blue, and Jessica wore yellow. She claims it was because she's against gender identification, but I'm pretty sure she just didn't read the invite.

All three of us walked up to the front door, which was obnoxiously covered in those plastic IT'S A BOY and IT'S A GIRL signs. My instinct was to vandalize them with "It's financial suicide with endless diarrhea," but I refrained. We all took one giant breath and opened the door into what was to become very similar to what I imagine an acid trip feels like.

The home was small, but it was an actual house. A grown-up house, in the suburbs, with a real-life white picket fence. My apartment in the city suddenly felt amateur and embarrassing in comparison. We walked in to find the home was packed with balloons, screaming babies, giant wedding rings, toys scattered on the floor doubling as little mini death traps, and the oddly familiar faces of high school classmates who had warped into humans pretending to be adults pretending to have a handle on their monsters pretending to be babies. My heart began to race. What would I say to these now strangers? How would I avoid conversations where I would inevitably reveal my clear disdain for love, marriage, and childbirth? I mean, seriously, do you know you shit yourself when you push that baby out? Your vagina rips and you SHIT yourself! I began to sweat. I wasn't ready. I wasn't prepared. I couldn't handle the accusing stares from these sexually frustrated parents. THEY knew I knew they hadn't had sex in months. I knew THEY knew I'd had sex the night before with that guy who lives on his ex-girlfriend's couch. Don't judge me—he was kind of cute, and she was out of town. Oh man, this wasn't going to end well. This couldn't end well. Was this ever going to end? And then, like the glorious light at the end of the tunnel that you read about in those weird hippie articles on Facebook where the guy comes back from the dead to tell us that he "SAW. THE. LIGHT," my eyes finally focused in on the most stunning sight I had ever seen...a fully stocked bar.

As fast as a teenager snapchats her frenemy giving the weird acne kid a hand job in the theater rafters at the Sadie Hawkins dance, Randi, Jess, and I raced to the bar. We filled our unusually large cups unusually high with unusually disproportionate amounts of vodka and downed them at an unusually fast pace. Ok, that last part was a lie. We pretty much always drink vodka at the speed of light. But finally...aah...that sweet booze relief. Just like that, with color in our cheeks, warmth in our hearts, and numbness in our heads, we finally felt like we could conquer this absurd gender-reveal celebration. We threw our arms in the middle of a huddle, like a team of...some sports reference. "One...two...three! Act like we care!" We tossed our hands up in the air with confidence and went our separate ways.

The next hour was filled with saturated small talk that ended in me making some inappropriate dick jokes, as I looked over at Randi, who was having a deep conversation with the dog in the corner. Jessica was spending her time drinking gin straight from the bottle with Grandma Jean, the only other reasonable human here. At some point, after my fifth time saying, "We just realized the only thing we really have in common is that we both like boys," the three of us found ourselves sitting crisscross applesauce in front of a two-year-old demon-child. She glared at us with hatred as we "goo-gooed" and "gah-gahed" because we didn't know how to do the baby thing. Her mom chuckled at us as she pointed out how smart her little angel was. I assumed she was implying that the little chunk was smarter than the three of us combined. At this point in our vodka marathon, I couldn't really disagree with her. The three of us stood up to go fill our cups one more time, and like any natural disaster that sneaks up on an innocent community just trying to live their single beautiful lives, that blob of a child PROJECTILE VOMITED right past us and ALL OVER the gender-reveal cake. It was like a horror movie in my head, played in slow motion. The orange-yellow-brown mixture clad with pieces of her soul arched up through the air while jaws dropped, hands shot out, and screams ensued.

I realize this was disheartening for everyone involved,

especially the soon-to-be parents who were dying to know what genitalia their kid was going to dangle around for the rest of their life. I certainly don't want to take away from the legit distress the mother of that kid blowing chunks probably felt in that moment. And I am sure everyone else at the party was freaked out too, praying their kid doesn't get whatever fucked-up kid sickness that was. (Seriously, kid sicknesses are insane. They get worms in their butts. Legit WORMS IN THEIR BUTTS.) I just felt these unavoidable feelings I couldn't properly process or maturely handle in that very moment. This party was a crash course in what the future held for me, and it threw me for a far bigger loop than I was prepared for. It's as if all my fears associated with change had been purposely placed right in front of me, in this gender party hell house, packed with judgmental peers, swirled together in a haze of vodka, topped with an explosion of baby barf. I know, the party wasn't about me, but my anxiety was rearing and there was no stopping it.

My stomach dropped. My palms were wet. My head began to spin. I COULDN'T DO IT ANY LONGER! Then, a switch flipped. With no regret, thought, or goodbyes, I BOLTED. I literally ran out of the house. Surely everyone saw me, but I couldn't help it. My body took over. I ran, Forrest Gump style, out of the house, down the long driveway, and then full speed down the street with tears in my eyes. It was all too much. Growing up. Changing paths. Feeling behind. It was too much, and all I could do was run. And run. And run. Halfway down the street, I stopped for a second to take a breather, because I'm not a damn runner; I'm a drinker. I could hardly breathe. Then, like music to my ears, I heard loud footsteps, crunching leaves, and heavy breathing behind me. I did a slo-mo turn, like they do in the movies, to reveal the loves of my life running toward me. Randi and Jessica, looking like professional drunken athletes, were sprinting my way. Quickly the tears in my eyes were overthrown by uncontrollable laughter as we all came together, huddled with hands on our knees, winded breaths, and smiles that filled our whole faces. Without words, we put our arms around each other, took a deep group breath, and walked down the street into the sunset. In that moment, we knew no matter how much life changed, we'd always have each other. We'd always be us.

For those who feel left with a gender cliff-hanger, the baby came out a boy who looks like a girl. Jessica wearing yellow actually ended up making the most sense. She always has fantastic dumb luck.

Not too long after that day, Randi told us that she was pregnant. She was beaming when she announced the news. She had wanted a baby for as long as I can remember, and if anyone should have one, it's her. She is the most educated on the subject; plus, the combination of her and her husband's looks makes for angel children. I couldn't have been happier for her, knowing this was her dream. I would be lying, though, if I said I didn't have a good old-fashioned meltdown in the car, after hearing the wonderful news. I felt like ten-year-old me, crying in the backseat of the car, desperately wanting to give my dog back. I wanted my best friend to have everything she ever wanted, but I didn't want things to be different. Our friendship was perfect—it was the one thing I could always rely on. Would Randi becoming a mom shift everything? Change had been happening all around us, but now it was happening to us. I wasn't sure I could handle it. I know that sounds so selfish, but in that moment, it was my truth.

Throughout the nine months of her pregnancy, I continued to worry about the pending changes, but even with the little shifts in routine (we didn't go out for drinks as much anymore, although Randi was a sober sport when we did), things felt just as great as they always had. I was learning to trust that regardless of the new additions or shifts we'd face, we would be ok.

Jessica and I were there the morning Randi gave birth to the most perfect son. The look of love in Randi's eyes was palpable, and all my worries were eased. How could your best friend being in complete bliss make you anything but perfectly happy? I held him and fell instantly in love, and with that love came an all-new phase of our friendship. Suddenly our nights out turned into the most fun nights in, watching the little man grow and learn. So much so that it was all we wanted to do, to the point that Randi had to remind us that she needed to leave the house once in a while. Now we go over and help feed him before taking Mommy out, because he's become part of our lives, and part of our friendship, and it's perfect.

Change is scary and hard and brain jiggling. Change

is also beautiful and exciting and elevating. It's just how you attack it and who you have with you during the battle. Choose your team wisely. I know not everyone is lucky enough to have childhood friends who are still their best friends. But you do have the power to keep the friends who support and grow with you and to let go of the ones that bring you down or hold you back.

Remember being in high school and the pressure you felt to make friends with the cool kids? At the time, you thought it was crucial to your success. You believed that you had to be in that group of pretty girls who all the other girls wanted to be and who all the boys wanted to be inside. You would go to extremes, like ditching your middle school best friend, just to achieve this goal that society had somehow drilled into your head. Then in college you were swamped by the stress of joining the best sorority. Paying for a group of doe-eyed, overenthusiastic, matching-outfit friends, even if it meant leaving your real friends at the dorm. Then, after eight years of relationships based on status, you realized you didn't have one true friend in the real world. What was the point?

My advice, if you want it, is stick with the friends you made in middle school, or the ones you befriended in the dorms, or anyone you have always been able to be your nerdy self around. Opt out of the popular route or the group you chose because you were afraid of not fitting in. Look for the friends with heart and loyalty. Humor and honesty. A willingness to communicate and grow. Friends who will come lie in bed with you when you are heartbroken. Friends who will be at the hospital in the wee hours of the morning to welcome your baby into the world. Friends who will hold your hand as you watch your relative go into the ground. Friends who will make any life change, like bringing home a new puppy, seamless. Or at least a hell of a lot easier. Most importantly—and I urge you to write this down—look for friends who will absolutely run out of a gender-reveal party after you when it all gets to be a little too much.

Peter Pan Fail

You're giving me the "It's not you, it's me" routine? I invented "It's not you, it's me"! Nobody tells me it's them, not me. If it's anybody, it's me!
—George Costanza

I found the love of my life on a dating app. He was every-thing I had always wanted but never thought I deserved. We spoke for hours on the phone every night until we finally met in person. It was more perfect than I could have ever imagined. We walked hand in hand as it magically started to snow. We stayed up all night listening to music, sharing tales of our past. We laughed till we cried watching Peter Pan–fail videos. (You haven't lived until you've witnessed at least three flying Peter Pans accidentally knock down an entire set.) We proclaimed our mutually strong feelings for each other, giggling like elementary school kids with a crush. We made the sweetest love and I fell asleep in his arms, feeling relieved, safe, and complete. I had found my person, my other half. It was the best night of my life.

I never saw him again.

This is internet dating.

My guess is you've experienced something just as devastating. Maybe you've been ghosted or you thought you were in a relationship that was far more serious than the other person believed. I think we can all agree that online dating is an unavoidable bitch, because what other choice do we have? Meet someone in real life? That requires getting dressed and leaving the house. Why would we do that when we can mindlessly swipe in our sweats, without a bra, curled up on the couch?

Here's the problem with internet dating, though: No one is accountable for their actions. It's a playground without rules, and honestly I understand the appeal. How fucking awesome would it have been if you were set loose in a toy store, told you can take whatever you want, and once you were done playing with one toy you could easily grab another? Beyond exciting, right? Now, as an adult, you can live out an equivalent fantasy; swipe an app for an ego boost but never respond back, chat until bored then abruptly stop without explanation, meet up with someone for a free drink then never see them again—all of this without any consequences. Let's be honest: It's selfish but totally attractive, especially for those times when you just want to take the easy way out. That's what apps were invented for in the first place, to make your life a little more effortless.

It's not just men that do this; I once went out with a guy simply because his profile said he was super handy.

It's not that I didn't like him—his company was pleasant enough—but there was no foreseeable future for us. What I did see in my immediate future, however, was him changing my light bulbs, patching some floor cracks, and repainting my walls. Once we ran out of rooms to fix, I conveniently ran out of time to see him. I still feel guilty about it, but my place looks great.

On the flip side, there have been times when I really wanted to take online dating seriously—when I didn't want to be a monster looking for shallow validation, and I'd swipe with sincere intentions instead of handing my phone to my married friends to let them "play." In those moments, I believed the app was a means to my "perfect end," and I craved accountability and stability, expecting the people on the app to suddenly desire the same. Romantic naiveté or selfish entitlement, assuming that just because I'm ready to be serious, everyone else should be too? I know it's probably the latter. It isn't until I take a seemingly perfect guy home for a good old-fashioned make-out session and he ends up leaving with my favorite pair of high heels hidden in his coat that I am brought back to the sobering reality that not everyone is dating for the same reasons. I'm not exaggerating, this actually happened. This guy was in it for the shoes—no joke. When I woke up the next morning, my heels were nowhere to be found. I texted him to poke around for information, but he never got back to me.

I have a couple of theories on what he did with them. One is that he has a "Wall of Conquests," a bookshelf displaying a variety of high heels from all the girls he's hooked up with via the internet. I like this theory because it reminds me of all my favorite crime shows, but I'm not dead. (I especially like that part.) My other theory is that he is currently strutting his stuff, in my heels, down Santa Monica Boulevard in the heart of West Hollywood. If this is the case, go get 'em, baby. Just, next time, it would be cool if you'd ask to borrow my shoes before leaving me in a quandary about the validity of dating apps.

This is just the tip of my online dating iceberg. Most of my stories are failures of titanic proportions, ending with me begging to go down with the ship. Maybe it's karma for the times I mindlessly fucked someone over, but I once went on a date with a guy who I had been talking to for a few weeks online that claimed to be a writer. It wasn't until I drilled him in person about his work that he finally admitted he worked as a mechanical bull operator at a trashy bar in Hollywood. I could have accepted that if he hadn't followed that reveal up with a two-minute rendition of Coldplay's "Yellow" on a harmonica that he had brought with him to the bar. I've never been the type to only have one drink, but you bet your ass I got out before the waitress even had time to offer a second.

I dated another guy I met online who was supercute, but he never had much to say, so we just got naked a lot. Around month four I suspected he was seeing someone else. I tried to confront him about it, but he adamantly denied it. I Sherlock Holmes'd the hell out of Instagram and found numerous pictures of him with some other chick who was clearly not just a work buddy. In spite of my findings, I kept the knowledge to myself and bought my friends and I tickets to see his band play at some fancy New Year's Eve celebration (a recurring mistake of mine, dating musicians). A few days before the big night, I texted him to ask some questions about the event, and he never responded. As in, NEVER responded. I ended up hanging at my apartment, with my friends, instead, talking shit about the dude into the New Year. We were blown away that not only did this dude ghost me but he ghosted all of my friends that night too. Even bolder, he came back around, texting me a few months later, asking to hang out, as if nothing ever happened. When I replied back in shock, questioning the New Year's ghosting, he adamantly contested it ever happened. I should have known from the clay pendant on a hemp rope he wore around his neck in his profile picture that this was not going to work out.

I also went on a date with a guy who asked me what I did for a living, and after I explained that I made videos on the internet, he looked me dead in the eyes and said (without an ounce of sarcasm), "Oh, so you're crazy?" I was so taken aback that I didn't have the wherewithal to properly respond. Lucky for me, a bird did and immediately took a shit on this dude's head. I sucked down my drink, asked for the check, and laughed the whole way home. Had that bird not taken that perfectly aimed crap on my behalf, I may have been more upset, but I counted that night as a win. After all, he wasn't wrong—I am crazy. We all are. Online dating breeds insanity; it's not our fault.

The most unnerving story, though, is the one I began this rant with. The man who I was convinced was the love of my life. I honestly can't figure out exactly what happened, and it still drives me nuts. With all these other guys, it was so cut-and-dried. An obvious lack of connection, a quick moment of bad judgment, an avoidance of accountability. Your textbook online dating scenarios. This was different, though, at least I was convinced it was, and it fucked with my brain for a very long time.

At the time, I had been online dating for a while. I was swiping left and right on every stupid app I drunkenly loaded on my phone, trying to get myself "back in the game" after recovering from a recent breakup. I had passed through every shirtless hunk, B-level actor, and bearded hipster profile there was. After a while they all became a blur, one self-employed bro (which always means unemployed) after another. Until him.

My heart stopped as he appeared on my screen. Think Rick Moranis meets Matthew Broderick (I have a thing for little nerdy Jews). I assume most girls passed him by, but I was stopped dead in my tracks. His face, serious. His glasses, round. His aura, familiar. I needed to know him; I HAD to know him. I hardly blinked before swiping right, and there it was: confirmed match. Butterflies fluttered in my stomach as I began to compose the message I was going to send him. I went back through his profile to try to find something I could cleverly comment on. I am not the "hi" only kind of girl; I'm an overachiever. In reviewing his profile, I realized I had failed to notice one crucial thing: He lived in New York City. Son of a bitch, that's real fucking far from me.

Humanity's propensity for making terrible decisions is the cash cow of the online dating industry. Without millions of people making poor choices and having to go back for more, the whole racket wouldn't exist. It thrives on us numb souls seeking constant endorphin rushes by way of empty conversations and dead-end hookups. I wasn't about to pass this terribly unrealistic situation up.

> Hi. You are so cute I failed to realize just how far away you are from me.

His reply came quickly, mirroring a similar sentiment, and with that, we began.

We started by batting conversation back and forth on the app, then to text, and within days, we were setting up a FaceTime date. (We were moving through the online dating bases FAST!) I realize this all sounds lame, but this is what dating in the modern era looks like. Nothing fantastical like the story of my grandpa meeting my grandma, who apparently experienced love at first sight. Well, Gramps did, after seeing Gram's picture in a local newspaper. She was crowned Miss June at her local dance hall. A couple of months later, my grandpa was at a dance and saw Miss June dancing with another man. Without any thought, he tapped the man on the shoulder and announced he was cutting in. They danced all night, and that was the beginning of their fifty-six-year-long love story. My story started with me sitting in LA with my phone in hand, waiting to get a FaceTime call from this stranger in New York.

When the phone rang, I quickly set it to a flattering angle, turned on the perfect light to blur my imperfections, took a deep breath, and pressed the green button. With the chime of the connection, there he was. Right in front of me, on my screen, but this time he was live. He was also wearing a matching pajama set like an old man, and I was instantly smitten.

Never had I met someone so confident in their quirky skin. He was small and neurotic, brilliant and unique. Most would say he was weird, but I would say he was perfect. That first night we talked for two hours, and then, every night thereafter. We would chat about our days; he would stop to play something he had written on the piano. I would tell him all the random things I think about, like how there must be someone on the other side of the planet taking a sip of their coffee at the exact same time I am or how insane it is that there are endless amounts of chickens in the world. How does every menu have chicken on it? Where the fuck do all these chickens come from? He would giggle and tell me he likes the way I think; he never judged me or made me feel strange for expressing myself. Our conversations were long but never forced. No subject was off-limits, and no conversation skimmed the surface. It was always intricate and personal, deep and satisfying. I was falling in love over the phone and nothing felt strange about it. We both agreed neither of us wanted to wait any longer to be together, so I booked my ticket to New York.

The day finally came; I landed at JFK and immediately hopped into a cab to meet Mr. Internet. Although we had spent many hours chatting and seeing each other on a screen, my heart was racing with nervous energy. Up to this point, everything about our connection was perfect, but the months of buildup leading to this moment added so much pressure. I put the expectation of walking in and instantly falling in love on myself because I wanted it so bad. I was praying this would all go as I had planned.

I arrived at the bar located at the bottom of the Midtown Manhattan hotel where I was staying. I knew I was looking for a small man with glasses and dark hair. I waltzed through the room, trying to feign confidence, glancing from table to table. Nothing brings me more anxiety than taking a lap around a bar in search of the person I'm supposed to meet. Everyone stares at you as you pace back and forth, wondering if you've been stood up. I moved briskly, hoping no one was watching me. Then I spotted him—the back of him. Dark hair, slim build, a nice coat. I gave myself a mental thumbs-up and tapped him on the shoulder.

"Well, hello," I said, oozing charm. My heart was practically beating out of my chest, and I felt like I was going to vomit.

"Umm," said the man as he turned and looked up at me.

My first reaction when I saw his face was I've been cat-fished into going on a date with a guy that doesn't look anything like his pictures. Although I was pretty certain this Asian man in his midfifties before me was not the man I had FaceTimed with for the last month.

"Oh, sorry," I said as I made a sharp turn away from his table with the little dignity I had left.

Then my face, now red from pure embarrassment, turned in the opposite direction, landing directly on him, the real him, sitting in a small booth. As I walked over, he raised his eyes to meet mine. We both smiled.

He stood up as I approached the table. He was way shorter than I had imagined, but lucky for both of us, I'm shorter than literally everyone, so it didn't matter. I wasn't sure if we were supposed to shake hands, hug, or high-five. I had been on so many first dates, but this was technically our twenty-third-ish date, so what's the protocol? I stood there awkwardly, unsure what do, until he went in for the double-cheek kiss. (Of course he's a worldly gentleman!)

"You are even prettier in real life," he said. With that, we were off.

At first, I was completely awestruck. I couldn't believe Mr. Internet was actually in front of me, not on a screen. It's a bizarre experience to meet someone you know so well but also not at all. I was well aware of his passion for music and his views on politics, but I was a stranger to the feel of his hands and lips. I was fully conscious of his insecurities and neuroses, but I was unfamiliar with what it was like to brush up beside him. The whole start of the night felt like I was relearning something I had never properly learned. I was visibly nervous and stumbled over my words, analyzing every moment as it was happening. I couldn't help but internally obsess, questioning if his expectations of how I was going to be in real life were fulfilled. I was so worried about what he thought about me I barely had a moment to form an opinion about him.

As the night continued, and the booze flowed, I slowly started to get out of my head. Without my constant inner monologue, I was able to engage like an actual human and enjoy Mr. Internet before me. Finally, the conversation was flowing seamlessly, as we tossed around our inside jokes. It felt natural and comfortable, like I was finally with the person I had come to know over the past few months. When we got up from the table to leave, he grabbed my hand, and suddenly we were us. With that one gesture of connection, everything fell into place. This was exactly what I was hoping for.

Knowing I was a huge theater nerd, he had gotten us tickets to see a Broadway show. He was the perfect gentleman, opening the door for me, holding my hand down the stairs, taking my coat off at our seats, and offering to get us drinks, because clearly this man was flawless. When he was off grabbing us cocktails, it occurred to me I had never been to a play on a first date. Mostly because I had never been out with such a thoughtful counterpart, but also the task always seemed daunting—sitting quietly next to a stranger, sharing in something that was so intimate and special to me. But when he returned, and the curtain rose, we sat hand in hand as if we had done this so many times before. It was my favorite Broadway show, and I don't even remember which one it was.

After the show, we decided to walk back to the hotel instead of taking a cab. Technically it was far enough away that a cab would have been more appropriate, but we both wanted to slowly stroll through the city. He told me he had made this walk so many times before, but the city never looked as pretty as it did with me by his side. I know, it sounds like a rehearsed line, but it felt like the most genuine proclamation in that moment. As we approached my hotel, it began to snow. I'm assuming if you are an East Coaster, this isn't anything too special, but to a native Southern California girl, it was magic. There I was, walking hand in hand with this incredible man, in the snow—I was in my own fairy tale. The only thing that could make it better is if he kissed me. Then, right on cue, he turned and did just that. Insert fireworks, cheesy music, and lady boners. It was pure enchantment.

He must have felt it too, sans the lady boner, because we made a U-turn and headed toward his place. He wanted to show me where he lived, and I wasn't about to turn down an invitation to get to see more of his life. I rarely go home with a man on the first date, but I could justify it this time. We had spent so much time "together" before this date it felt like it equated to whatever is an acceptable number of dates to go home with someone. Also, I was on "vacation," and regular rules don't apply on vacation. Neither do calories, but I can't seem to get my body to understand that one.

I know you aren't supposed to judge a book by its cover, but I do judge a man I met on the internet by his place. I don't require anything fancy, just something clean and uniquely his. Nothing is more terrifying than an apartment filled with nothing but IKEA furniture and empty walls. That's a recipe for a serial killer. Or worse, a man without a job.

As I stepped into Mr. Internet's Brooklyn apartment, I was overjoyed to find a home suited for this delightful genius. His walls were filled with framed sheet music, books were stacked in perfectly random piles, there was a piano positioned to entertain, and a vintage phonograph in the corner. Everything was in the right spot, but none of it seemed contrived. His bedroom was just the same—a wall of books and unique trinkets, a gun from the Civil War, a signed letter from Mel Brooks, a yo-yo from the White House. I had hit the quirky-guy jackpot!

Our night continued on with more fun talks that turned to deeper romantic conversations, which led to us making very sweet love. I realize I'm suddenly being coy about sex, but this time was different. It was sweet and passionate, kind and slow. I prefer to keep the rest to myself because some things are meant to be mine and mine only.

What I will share is our après sex. Which, I know isn't an actual term, but postcoital sounds too formal and also disgusting. Most men I had been with would jump in the shower or fall asleep after, but all he wanted to do was hang out and spend more time with me. I was leaving early the next morning and it would be a while until we saw each other again. We sat at his desk and rummaged through old photos he had and watched old videos I had made, anything and everything to help us dive deeper into each other.

Then, it happened. We entered into the delicious black hole of Peter Pan–fail videos. I don't know who initiated it or how it happened, but it did and it was everything I never knew I wanted. Set pieces falling, Peter Pans crashing, Nanas taking dumps on the stage. It was my own personal heaven, and to my surprise, it was his too. Never would I have imagined that this would be the moment that did it. I was completely myself, no makeup, no Spanx, full-on snort laughing, and I had, in fact, fallen in love with Mr. Internet.

I never saw him again. He promised he would come out to see me, but he never did. Our daily conversations turned into weekly ones, which then turned into "I can't talk right now" texts. I couldn't understand what was happening, so I constantly tried to seek answers. I was left with "we are too far apart" type responses, to which I desperately declared I would move to New York for him. This was insane, I am aware, and it was also the final straw that pushed him away.

For months after, I would stalk his social media, or text him randomly, trying to figure out if he had met someone else. I just needed to find something tangible that would help explain his sudden change of heart. I never got a response from him and couldn't find any proof of another woman. Finally, I had to force myself to accept the reality that Mr. Internet was nothing more than a blip on the internet-dating history timeline. A fleeting moment.

I eventually got back on the dating apps after recovering from my heartache. Some days I would use them with purpose; others I would swipe mindlessly. At one point, I was engaging in a conversation simply out of boredom when it clicked. Mr. Internet wasn't a bad man—his feelings for me may have even been sincere—but he was using the app for a completely different reason than I was. I'm not entirely sure what his intentions were (sex, company, someone to say good night to?); it doesn't matter now. The fact was we were on different pages, and I failed to realize it. Yes, he may have led me on, and I wish he had been clearer with what he wanted. However, I was so wrapped up in creating my perfect love story I never stopped to ask him if he wanted the same.

This is all to say, don't online date. Just kidding; I still wholeheartedly endorse meeting someone online, and I would never tell you to leave your house if you don't have to. I'm just reminding you that everyone on those apps is there for different reasons, and without accountability, it's hard to avoid the flops. So, if you are serious about finding someone to genuinely connect with, you have to treat it like a full-time job. Know what you want, be forthright with your questions, and listen carefully to the answers. Go out on dates, read between the lines, walk away if he pulls out a harmonica. Realize you'll meet many duds, expect crazy stories, but remain optimistic because there is someone out there with the same intentions as you. It may just take a million swipes to find them.

I don't regret falling in love with Mr. Internet, even if it was fleeting. That was one of the best nights of my life. I do regret the amount of energy I spent obsessing, for months after, trying to figure out what had happened. So much time wasted, when in the end, the only thing I figured out was this is just the way internet dating goes. So, I swipe on and hope for the best. Worst case, my heart gets broken again. Best case, a Peter Pan–fail viewing is just the start of a perfectly requited love story.

Water Cooler Conversations Are Real

I'm a great quitter. It's one of the few things I do well.

—George Costanza

Six a.m., my alarm blaring. My eyes whip open as I drag myself upright. In a complete panic, I rack my brain to remember what day it is and why my alarm is going off so early. I've always been a morning person, but 6 a.m. is pushing it. Then I remember: It is my first day of my "grown-up" job in a "grown-up" office with a "grown-up" dress code. I roll out of bed, chug as much coffee as I can without inducing an ulcer, and get into my car for the morning commute. The butterflies and first-day jitters quickly subside when I turn onto the 405 and am introduced to morning traffic. Growing up in Los Angeles, I am no stranger to gridlock, but morning-commute traffic is its own grizzly beast. It suddenly feels like I am on a never-ending cross-country flight with some obnoxious kid sitting behind me, continuously kicking my seat. Except there are no movies or booze to keep my anxiety at bay.

Just me, my thoughts, and hundreds of other disgruntled humans trying to get to their lackluster jobs. This is my introduction to being a responsible adult in the working world—slow and aggravating.

I finally understand why road rage exists; it provides a focal point for your frustrated energy. Sitting mindlessly in bumper-to-bumper traffic, knowing the light at the end of the tunnel is just a shitty day job that underpays and overworks, can drive a person to insanity. Blaming the traffic via a honk and an aggressive middle finger serves as a temporary Band-Aid to all of life's disappointments for at least a good twenty seconds. The rest of the time is filled with sighs and groans as you tune into the latest political befuddlings on the radio, or listen to some gruesome true-crime podcast, which ironically is far easier to digest.

After months of making this monotonous commute, my brain began to subconsciously drift into a dreaded existential helix where the radio sounds were overtaken by the noise of my panicked inner monologue. *How did I get here? This wasn't the dream I set out for myself. Why am I wearing a cardigan?* And the most frightening—*am I turning into my father?*

Before you worry, Dad, because I know you're reading this, let me explain. My father is the definition of a hard worker. Told at a young age by his teachers that he wouldn't amount to anything, he has worked tirelessly his whole life to fight that terrible false premise. He graduated from law school, started his own family law firm, argued before the Supreme Court twice, won both times, and was able to support our crazy family. An intense creature of habit, fueled by equal parts passion and fear of failure, he wakes up at 6 a.m., drives an hour to work, fights *with* people, eats the same lunch at the same restaurant at the same time, fights *for* people, drives an hour home, eats the same dinner in the same chair at the same time, and repeats the next day. He is the poster child for "the daily grind," and he's the best at what he does. He is the ultimate example of how you should never let anyone tell you you're not good enough.

Like most men of his generation, Dad's a diligent motherfucker (disturbingly literal). I like to think I have a similar work ethic, convincing myself every day that 4:15 p.m. is almost 5 p.m., which means it's an appropriate time to drink an inappropriate amount of alcohol. That's hard work, you guys. However, my dad's commitment is based on more than proving his abilities; it's in his blood. His ancestors immigrated to America from Russia with nothing but an insanely strong desire to create good lives for themselves and their family. They believed wholeheartedly that if they dressed the part and worked hard, they would be respected and successful. Probably without even realizing it, my dad has carried these beliefs with him since the time he was old enough to get a job. Not surprising to either of us, although probably disappointing to him, I did not inherit such convictions. While he wears a suit to work every day and is highly regarded by the legal community, I wear sweatpants most days and rack up hate comments on YouTube. Carrying on his law legacy was clearly not in my charts.

Still, I yearned for his approval, and so when I was little, I may have led him on by telling him I wanted to be a lawyer like him when I grew up. I wonder now if there was justification for my desperation, or if that's just a built-in father/daughter thing. I guess I felt the need to keep everyone happy in my family. I'm the self-appointed family glue, fielding my parents', grandparents', and brother's emotions. At a young age, I could sense my father wanted my brother to follow in his footsteps—play sports, join a fraternity, become a lawyer. But that wasn't my brother, and we all knew it right away. He's an introverted intellectual, whose path to becoming a professor in some tucked-away town set in well before puberty struck. So early on, I took it upon myself to try to fill that void in my dad, and I did it by fronting that my dreams were his dreams.

The truth is that for as long as I can remember, all I've ever wanted to be when I "grew up" was an actor. The desire began when I was five or six years old and I watched my cousin perform in *Grease* at the local children's theater. Maybe it was the sound of the audience cheering, or the almost on-pitch singing, or the costumes that looked as if they'd never been washed that I'd still kill to wear, but whatever it was, I was hooked.

I remember so distinctly going home that night and dreaming about performing on that rickety, completely not-child-safe stage. The fact that I can remember this so clearly is odd because my therapist asks me about my childhood all the time and I often have trouble recalling the majority of it. She thinks it's because I had some trauma that I have since shoved under the proverbial rug, but I think it's the fact that I mixed Xanax and booze one too many times in college. Literally, nights would go by and I would have no recollection of them. (Thanks, parents, for paying for my tuition. I learned a lot, I swear. I just blacked most of it out.) Yet this dream I had that night after my cousin's show is still so perfectly lucid. I was Sandy, singing on that stage, with all the lights hitting my face as the audience went wild. It was a rush, a magical feeling, and I woke up convinced it was all I ever wanted to do.

By the time I was seven, my mom, knowing that my passion for law was really just a cry for daddy's approval, signed me up to audition for that same theater program my cousin had done. I think it was her way of saying it was ok for me to pursue my real dreams. Or, it was her "fuck you" to the justice system. Either way, I'm glad she did. I remember it so vividly, as if a Xanax martini had never entered my body. I stood in my mom's bathroom in a blue-and-white jumpsuit, my hair pulled back in a migraine-inducing bun as she put lipstick on me, like the most committed pageant mom. I took a deep breath, smiled at my reflection in the mirror, and uttered, "This is what you're meant to do." I may have been new to acting, but I was no stranger to dramatics.

I got into our '87 Volkswagen. You know, the one with the seats in the trunk that popped up. I always got so carsick when I sat back there, but the constant nauseated feeling was worth the chance of seeing someone famous head on. Growing up in LA, this was of course a common occurrence, and I loved it. Not because I wanted to meet them; I just wanted to BE them. One time we were driving down Ventura Boulevard, stopped at a red light, and we saw Rick Dees behind us. Mr. KISS FM himself! My brother and I gave him a thumbs-up, and like a good celebrity, he shot one right back at us. I mean, would Ryan Seacrest do that? Eh, probably. He seems insanely starved for attention, and I mean that in the best way possible. That guy is a work machine—he never stops. Seriously, when does he have time to poop? I'm honestly concerned for his bowels. I can't poop unless I take the time to wake up, have coffee, sit for a good twenty minutes—or as an ex once called it, "perch"—and then stalk people on Instagram as I drop last night's meal off. (Sorry to break it to you, but girls poop.)

I'm telling you, though, if I don't go through the whole damn routine first thing in the morning, I won't go for the whole day. You think I'm exaggerating, but when I went on my Birthright trip to Israel, which is basically just a free twelve-day party for twenty-something-year-old Jews, I didn't poop once. Oprah says this is common when traveling, but Oprah for sure hasn't gone twelve days without taking a dump. You know she would pay to have someone pump poop out of her if she went more than twenty-four hours without a release. Is that what Ryan Seacrest does? Otherwise, I don't know how he manages it.

I didn't have that luxury in the Holy Land, so I just kept shoving hummus in my mouth, hoping for the red seas to part in my colon and release a miracle. No such luck. Another mystery my therapist attributes to a childhood trauma. I'm not sure why I continue paying her. I'm going broke and still can't poop in public bathrooms.

Anyway, as Mom and I pulled up to the theater, which was just a beat-up auditorium at the middle school in the next town over, I began to freak out. Everything I wanted was right in front of me, but I was frozen in my seat. Seeing the fear quickly take over my little mind and body, my wonderful mom shoved me out of the car and drove away. (The line between child abuse and good parenting is often so slim.) With that, I reluctantly made the first steps toward what would be the rest of my life.

Now, I am certainly not an overnight success. Not even an Emma Stone à la *La La Land* kind of success. Because, one: I think that movie's overrated. Two: She is way more successful than me. Three: I was cast as a Munchkin that day and it's been a VERY slow climb ever since.

That has never stopped me from working at a Ryan Seacrest obsession level, though. I'd like to thank self-motivation for my work ethic, but the reality is I guilted myself into it. That self-imposed fear of potentially letting my father down continued to stalk me, as I inched further into my twenties, like a dog begging for the last bite of bacon. I wanted to make that pup happy, but I fucking love bacon. What's a girl to do? My answer: cut the last bite in two so both of us might hopefully be satisfied. I would pursue my dream of being an actor while also taking on a million jobs to prove that I was hardworking like him and ease his fears of having to financially support me forever.

My brain wasn't naturally capable of working a regular nine-to-five job, which was one of the many stereotypes from a BuzzFeed "Are You Actually a Millennial" quiz I deeply related to. That and using your significant other's Netflix and Hulu log-in. What's the point of being in a relationship otherwise? I avoided full-time jobs because I had to leave my days open for the auditions I never got, and I was adamant about not waiting tables, for no other reason than not wanting to become a cliché. These ridiculous parameters obviously limited my options and resulted in me taking a bizarre series of part-time jobs to support myself while pursuing my childhood dreams.

I was a birthday party entertainer, which is a fancy way of saying I spent my days as a clown. My duties included navigating through Los Angeles via printed-out MapQuest directions (RIP), dressing up in whatever costume was handed to me that morning—praying the Lysol smell wasn't in lieu of laundering—and showing up to a stranger's home hoping I didn't get killed. Oh, and I had to keep the kids entertained. That was always last on my agenda. (For the record, I don't think I have a biological clock, but more to come on that later.)

For a few months, I was hired as a personal assistant to a sixteen-year-old, which is fancier than anything I've ever said. I was basically hired to aid her in activities that her parents should have been doing with her themselves. Like, teaching her how to drive, which is probably on my top-ten-scariest-things-I've-ever-done list, just below smoking weed on the porch of a brothel in Jamaica. I also took her to auditions that I would have killed to have gotten in on. (Please note: Never use the word "kill" when smoking weed at a brothel in Jamaica.) The worst part: I had to talk her through her social-life issues, which were far more interesting than anything happening in my lame life. (Besides the stoned Jamaica brothel extravaganza, obviously.)

There was a long period of time when I worked as a beer and liquor promo model, which sounds cool but it just meant I had to stand in front of the fridge section in the grocery store and peddle free nonalcoholic samples with coupons. It was beyond humiliating and freezing. Most of the time people would walk past me and avoid eye contact, as if I were just another Red Bull can they didn't want to buy because they've finally realized Red Bull can't give you wings, just potential heart attacks. Sometimes dudes would hit on me because they assumed if I was lame enough to take the job, I might be lame enough to date them. The most memorable interaction was the elderly lady who came up to me and told me that the booze I was promoting would cause the baby inside me to come out as the devil. I wasn't sure which I was more offended by—the fact that she didn't want the coupon or that she thought I was pregnant.

All these jobs temporarily filled my days, my rent checks, and the void I felt in my acting career, but after years of weird part-time job after weird part-time job, I was exhausted and defeated. I had hardly advanced as an actor, unless you consider one student film and a YouTube music video progress, and I was still trying to convince my dad (and myself) that I was on the right track. I was down on my luck, living paycheck to paycheck, completely embarrassed by my pursuits, when I got a call from Yahoo Studios.

It was like the nine-to-five gods knew they could get me when I was down, so they offered me a position as their in-house host. The job was disguised as an acting gig, even though it only required me to read the news off a teleprompter, but the truth was it was a corporate job, in a corporate office, on a corporate schedule. Sure, I was pushing my dreams aside for the corporate life, but that corporate paycheck seemed like a decent substitute for the time being.

Upon accepting the job, I immediately called my dad to share the news. After he cross-examined me for details, specifically the financial ones, he exploded with pride. (You would have thought I told him I won the lottery and decided to give it all to him as a massive IOU check after years of abusing his Mastercard). His level of excitement floated me to the "I'm not a fuckup" clouds, and I wanted to live in that place for as long as I could.

To be honest, I think my dad was mostly excited because now someone in the family could finally understand the pure hell that he'd been living all these years. He of course disguised this sick pleasure with the ruse that he was just happy to have someone to chat with for an hour while we both sat in miserable traffic at 7 a.m. Many mornings he would call, so fucking chipper for a man who doesn't drink coffee, and belt out Dolly Parton's "9 to 5" as if I found it amusing. The only thing I found amusing was how off-key he was. He's like the William Hung of our family. No rhythm, no voice, no shame. Poor William Hung, the butt of everyone's jokes. What do you think he's doing now? I just Googled him; I couldn't resist. He rode his *American Idol* fame for a few years and once that sad ride came to a halt, he became an administrative assistant for the Los Angeles County Department of Public Health. He bangs no more, according to his LinkedIn page.

It didn't take long for me to settle into the corporate life and, subsequently, a depression. What I had told myself would be a short-term gig turned into two years of commuting and playing the nine-to-five game to keep my dad impressed. My acting dreams were muted, my gas tank got more action than me, and I had fallen into a routine that I had begun to accept as my "path."

There are a lot of things about office life that I didn't know until I was knee-deep in it. Things I feel like people should warn you about so you are fully prepared when you enter into this chapter of your life. For instance:

1. The people working alongside you are miserable. They may smile and wave, but it's just their way of trying to stop you from killing yourself, because they have the same desire.

2. Your bosses may seem like they have their shit together, but they're really just terrified of their own bosses.

3. All offices blast their air-conditioning to freeze the germs and your soul. Seeing people in full-on parkas in the middle of summer is the norm. Don't forget yours.

4. People take donut-day very seriously. You've never seen a group of mundane people light up as much as they do at the sight of that pink box. Don't even try to reach for the coveted bear claw. Larry in Accounting staked his claim on it years before you arrived and will stop at nothing for the claw. Have you seen Tina in Sales? She didn't always have a missing thumb.

5. The bathroom is the only safe place. It's a quiet sanctuary where you can sit alone and hide out from the miserable, industrial carpeted hell waiting for you outside the door. If you can find a one-person bathroom, you've hit the jackpot. Lock the door and claim diarrhea. Great way to kill an hour.

6. The encouraging signs posted on the walls from Corporate are ploys to make you believe they care about you. Don't let the ethnically ambiguous man jumping for joy, shouting, "I'm part of a team!" fool you. You are just a puppet in their moneymaking scheme, and you will never be able to jump as high as that dude on the poster.

7. Facebook is for people who sit at a desk all day. If you're lucky, you'll have a date you need to pre-stalk, which could take you on a several-hour journey into the social media abyss. I once landed on a date's ex-girlfriend's fifth cousin's ex–best friend's sister's middle child's mistress. Call me if you need help stalking.

8. If you don't clean out your food from the office fridge on Friday, some uptight, sweater-wearing, rule-following lunatic is going to be so pissed at you. That passive kind of pissed that results in sticky notes on the fridge for the rest of eternity that say, "This is a community; do YOUR part," and "We're all adults; clean up after yourself."

9. Going out for drinks with your workmates is always a bad idea. It may seem like a fun idea at the time because you are desperate to blow off steam after being cooped up in a maze of cubicles, and the bar across the street is having two-dollar taco night, but beware. The only thing worse than being at work is talking about work, which is hard to avoid when it's the only real common thread between your co-workers. It's a major buzzkill, not to mention two-dollar tacos will always give you the poops. All that aside, you DO NOT want to see Gary from Marketing drunk. Trust me. It will get to so many levels of weird, and then you have to deal with weeks of uncomfortable run-ins every time you pass by him in the kitchen.

10. This brings me to my last discovery, which I once thought was something you would only see in the movies or on TV, but I was wrong. Water cooler conversations are real. I repeat, water cooler conversations are real. You can't avoid them, and in fact, you may even find yourself indulging in them because you've been sucked into the office culture, and there is no escaping the mindless conversation with that weird dude from HR about the latest viral-video star Ellen made dance on her TV show, while you water your parched office-worker soul. You, my friend, are the cliché.

One day I found myself wandering into the Yahoo office kitchen for the fourteenth time in a two-hour span to kill time and graze the snacks. I forgot to mention that working in an office makes you fat. I figured that was just a known fact. Anyway, in an attempt to hydrate my sodium-filled body thanks to the endless amount of cashews provided by the establishment to cure boredom, I went to fill my water bottle up at the water cooler. It was just then that another business casual–clad lemming came over and leaned against the cooler. Faster than you can say, "Help! I have social anxiety and I don't want to have to think of something to say!" we were in a full-on conversation about the weather. THE FUCKING WEATHER! It's not that he wasn't nice, and to be fair it was interesting that we were having rain in Los Angeles, because it never rains in Los Angeles, but as I stood there nodding my head and preparing for the moment when he would surely pull out pictures of his kids and I'd have to gush over them and follow up with a story about my godbabies because I always try so awkwardly hard to relate, I realized that I had given in to living a version of my life I had once so desperately tried to avoid.

I quickly grabbed my half-empty water bottle, because at that moment there was no way I could fathom seeing it as half-full, and bolted to the bathroom. In a sweaty panic, I splashed water on my face, looked into the mirror, and thought, WHAT THE FUCK AM I DOING HERE?! This was not the career I dreamed of. Where was the little girl who stood in front of her Cabbage Patch dolls practicing acceptance speeches? Or the teenager who made all her friends audition for her so she could produce a killer version of *A Chorus Line* in the backyard? Where was the young lady who refused to take the easy route and preferred to fight for her dreams even if that meant dressing up like a clown for one lonely man's birthday?

I commend the people who can pull off the nine-to-five life, and salute those who enjoy that stability. It wasn't me, though, and it was never going to be me. No matter how much money I made or how proud I thought my dad was, I could never accept the corporate life as my forever life. I decided then and there, with water dripping down my face, that I'd much rather work a million odd jobs to make ends meet than let that windowless pit crush my soul one uncreative day at a time. I wanted to make things that inspire people, not spin around in a desk chair counting the minutes till the day was over. I wanted to make money as a result of doing what I love, not from clocking in and out. I wanted to work on my own timeline, not strictly between the hours of nine and five. Most importantly, I wanted to look in the mirror every day and be able to say to myself, "This is what you're meant to do," like I did with such certainty all those years ago. Instead, in that moment, I blurted out, "YOU CAN'T DO THIS ANYMORE!" at my reflection in the mirror, and to Marsha in PR who I didn't realize had been in the stall next to the sink the whole time.

Needing a second opinion, I reluctantly called my dad to let him know I was thinking of quitting my job so I could pursue a career I actually wanted. My heart raced as I waited for his response, which I assumed would be some combination of disagreement and disappointment. To my surprise, without skipping a beat, he replied, "I think it's a good idea, Bug. I just want you to be happy." There was no tone of dismay, not an ounce of dissent, just 100 percent pure love and support of me, my decisions, and my dreams. It was then that I realized how blind I had been all these years. It was never about following in his footsteps or making tons of money. I never had to pretend to like football or aspire to stand in court in order to impress him. My dad has always been proud of me, unconditionally. I was just too busy worrying myself to death to even notice. Everything I had been carrying on my shoulders for so many years was put there by me, and only me, and I was finally ready to let it go. What's the point of living if you are living for someone else? Or in my case, what you've imagined someone else wants?

A few days later, I quit. I packed up my desk, put the rest of my lunch in the fridge with the sticky note asking me not to, took the only bear claw, and busted out of that building for the last time. It felt good, real good.

I never looked back, never missed working there, and think very rarely about those two years. Now I'm working on things I'm passionate about, and it feels right. (Literally, I don't have to wear pants to work—YouTuber perks.) I do, however, miss one thing about that time. No, not the cashews—those made me fat and gassy even though they were delicious. What I miss is the morning phone calls with my dad. Complaining about the commute, talking about the latest Netflix show, and mostly, hearing him sing "9 to 5." It may have been off-key, but it kept me smiling, even in traffic. I love you, Dad. Thanks for always supporting me and my dreams.

My Denim Security Blanket

I see you're still sticking with the denim.
—Elaine Benes

overalls
noun—over·alls—\ˈō-vər-ˌȯlz\

Merriam-Webster Definition:
Loose protective trousers worn over regular clothes.

Lisa Schwartz Definition:
The "go-to" baggy piece of clothing that is more acceptable than sweats but still hides all your insecurities.

The day I turned thirty-two, I went with my mom to Nordstrom for our birthday tradition, lunch and shopping (we're basic bitches). After a glass of champagne and salad with dressing on the side—because even on my birthday I don't dare ask for the dressing "tossed in"—we headed out to shop. Within seconds, my eyes landed on the most beautiful article of clothing I ever did see.

"No way. You wore those all the time when you were a kid. I can't believe they're even selling them here. You cannot."

"Oh, I can, Queen, and I WILL!" I announced with pride. By now my mom was snort laughing at an impressively high volume.

I grabbed the pair of overalls hanging before me and took them right to the counter, no need to try them on. I knew they'd fit, because they've always fit. That's why I love them. It's like reuniting with an old friend you haven't seen in ages, but the minute you are together it feels as though no time has passed at all. Overalls were my best friend growing up, but even more than that, they were my baggy denim security blanket. They were my shield from the world being able to see my love-handled belly and my less-than-dainty thighs. They were the cure to my anxiety, relieving the stress of getting ready for school every morning, which was often too much for my neurotic mind to handle. They were my "go-to" outfit as a kid trying so hard not to look chubby, my cover-up to all my self-proclaimed flaws.

The moment I was reunited with them, that deep bonded feeling flooded right back in. Knowing overalls were back in style was the best 32nd birthday gift I could have ever received.

I had been struggling to find clothes that I felt comfortable in ever since I entered my thirties. Why didn't I bother to realize that your body does, in fact, change once you say goodbye to your twenties? It's not that you immediately turn back into a pumpkin—which is quite literally what I looked like as a child—it just gets exponentially harder to get your body to do what you want it to do. Suddenly hairs start growing in places that were once smooth. Lines begin appearing on your face that send you into a lotion-buying panic. Your metabolism refuses to speed up in order to handle the bag of chips and salsa you stress-ate the night before. Your weight redistributes itself to places you never thought it could. Overnight, your arms get thicker, your waistline expands, and extra junk magically gets added to your trunk. I know the last part doesn't sound all that bad, but those additions don't come in Beyoncé form. They're more of the "my clothes no longer fit even though I'm working out like a crazy person, and now I'm so beyond pissed because I need to buy all new clothes but I don't really have the money. Plus, I can't bear the thought of trying them on only to solidify I hate everything on this new old body" variety. Not to mention, your damn hips spread, prepping themselves to bear children. Not sure why they didn't check in with me about that first. There's absolutely no need to prep—I don't want a baby right now! Give me my old body back or at least more overalls to cover all this shit up.

To add more fuel to my insecure fire, after I hit thirty-two, I became single for the first time in years, so I had to deal with getting naked in front of new dudes with my new body. No amount of liquor would prepare me for that. I remember I was dating this guy on and off for six months, who was less than kind with his words (that's putting it nicely). Why do we as women put up with that stuff? My therapist is still working on helping me answer that. I'm certain I've paid off both of her kid's college tuitions at this point.

Anyway, I remember lying naked in his bed after we had just made love, minus the love part. He popped up and looked in the mirror. I was jealous of the way he was admiring himself. He never looked at me like that.

"Can you tell I've been working out?" he asked as he flexed.

"Um. Yeah. You look great," I said, as I literally lay there naked, praying he would turn around and tell me I looked beautiful.

"You have a happy trail." He pointed to the hair on my stomach stretching from my belly button to my pubic bone.

Before I could respond, he left the room and got into the shower. Ladies and gentlemen, this really fucking happened. Be careful who you swipe right on. You have been warned.

I hadn't noticed until just then that I'd grown hair there. Another fun little present my age had given me that I now pluck out regularly. I quickly got up, put on my clothes, and got the hell out. I wonder if he even noticed I'd left. My guess is he's still looking in the mirror. I hope he and his reflection have a great life together.

This isn't meant to make you feel bad for me or make you afraid of getting older. I just wish someone had told me that the hashtag "ITGETSBETTER" doesn't apply to the female body over age thirty.

When I went into production for my show *Party Girl*, I was working out obsessively and eating minimally. You would have thought I was training for some Miss America bikini contest, but I was just trying not to hate the way I looked in my costumes. On the first day, as I visibly shook in the makeup chair, frightened that I wouldn't be able to deliver what I had convinced everyone that I could as an actor, the makeup room door flung open, and in came an actress, in her fifties, who I had looked up to for as long as I can remember. I knew she was in the show, but at this point I hadn't met her. Of course, being the overthinker that I am, I'd already prepared a ton of things to say to her, but before I could even say hello, she blurted out to the entire room:

"I HAVE GAINED WEIGHT!"

"Shit. So, you're telling me it doesn't get easier?" I asked.

"It only gets harder," she said with a laugh.

From that point on, we were best buds. I also realized I needed to be a little gentler with myself because I'm in it for the long haul and this is the only body I've got.

I've never had the greatest metabolism to begin with, and for as long as I can remember, I've been on some sort of diet. I still have warlike flashbacks of my mom taking me, when I was nine, to see a nutritionist. She worked in a very small, windowless office deep in the Valley. The space resembled those I see on episodes of *Hoarders*, but instead of mountains of Slurpee cups and rat droppings, she had food pyramid posters and plastic produce stacked to the ceiling. The nutritionist appeared as if she hadn't eaten for days; I was hungry just looking at her. I remember sitting in the chair across from her as she held out her palm to show me the ideal serving size of protein I should be rationing to myself. As if nine-year-old me was preparing her own steak dinners. She also made me hold the plastic carrots to encourage me to eat more veggies. I'm pretty sure I didn't listen to a thing that frail bird said. Not because I didn't care, but because the sound of my tears and self-loathing overpowered her chirps.

I just wanted so badly to be like all the other girls my age. As I saw it, not only were they skinny but they could eat whatever they wanted, never worrying about portions or calories. I felt unfairly chubby and hated having to watch every damn thing I put in my mouth. I remember having multiple meltdowns as my mom would prep me for a birthday party, reminding me to watch my pizza intake. She was just trying to help me, but I was beyond upset that I couldn't "have fun" and eat like everyone else. I don't know what her solutions were in these moments, other than to buy me more overalls so at least I had something I felt secure in to wear. My poor mom; I can only imagine the amount of stress this put on her.

When I was ten, I got the role of Dorothy in *The Wizard of Oz*. I can still clearly picture my then-self in the costume, looking mega porky. Honestly, I looked like three Judy Garlands pushed into one gingham smock. I laughed as I reminisced about this with my mother over drinks the other night, and she proceeded to tell me that the owner of the theater pulled her aside after a rehearsal and told her, "If she doesn't stop eating candy, she will never fit into the costume." I had never heard that story before, and it shook me to my fat-kid core. Even as I write it, my heart is dropping into my not-so-flat stomach. Apparently, my mom responded by shouting, "Stop fucking selling fucking candy at the fucking theater to the fucking kids!" Which prompted us to order another round of drinks and celebrate her badassery.

When I was old enough, my mom started taking me along with her to Weight Watchers meetings. Nothing like counting calories to drive a young person to binge eat. I always hated math, so you expect me to not only count beyond the number of fingers on my hands but also deprive myself of dessert because I blew all my points on that Hot Pocket I had after school to make me feel better about Danny Berdakian calling me fat in history class? Still, I'd show up at 8 a.m. every Saturday with my mom to "weigh in." Fourteen-year-old me with a bunch of middle-aged hens.

In the nineties, nonfat was the huge new diet trend. You could eat all the frozen yogurt you wanted, as long as it was "nonfat." I was pounding nonfat cookies and cream, with a side of chemicals I couldn't pronounce, left and right. Another popular diet trend was my short-term best friend, Olestra. A fat substitute that adds no fat, calories, or cholesterol to foods. Instead, it makes you shit your brains out, "allegedly." Weight Watchers cleverly omitted that detail when promoting it. My mom and I purchased barrel upon barrel of Pringles with Olestra, and let's just say I spent most of eighth grade in the bathroom.

After graduating from high school as a Lifetime Member of Weight Watchers, I headed to college. I had been warned about the freshman fifteen from the ladies in my Saturday meetings, but with an unlimited meal plan to the dorms and endless pizza and fries, there was no chance I would walk away without tripling my size. Even the smallest humans are bound to expand to blimp-size versions of themselves—remember this. Ice cream, pancakes, fried anything at your disposal every day, all day?! It was better than Christmas. Or at least what I assume Christmas is like. Our Christmases consisted of us piling into my dad's car and driving down Ventura Boulevard to see which businesses were open. I'm not sure why we did that. I think my dad just liked to assess the percentage of other Jews in the neighborhood. We did a follow-up count one Christmas night at the Chinese restaurant. The whole neighborhood was there—my dad was very pleased.

Right before I broke for summer vacation after my freshman year of college, my parents conference-called me in my dorm room to tell me they were going to get a divorce. I listened in silence, hung up my flip phone, ate a microwaved burrito in record time, and decided I was going to spend the rest of my college years avoiding going home so I didn't have to deal with the reality of their deci-sion. I was so hurt by their spilt, not considering it was the healthy choice for them, that I continued to live on cam-pus and eat my way through the next three years. Round-ing out those college years, and my belly, I had gained far too much weight for my five-foot-one frame to be healthy. I legit looked like I was in a fat suit that some award-winning Hollywood special-effects artist worked hours on to achieve. In actuality, it just took me three years of emotional late-night snacking. Quite an accomplishment.

When I graduated, I couldn't afford my own place, so I moved back into my childhood home, which was now only inhabited by my father. It was a very surreal experience, for after avoiding being there for the past three years, it felt like a frat house version of the home I used to know. At first glance, everything was the same—the old furni-ture, the eighties decor, the pictures on the walls—but when I looked closer, I began to notice distinct bachelor pad changes. The pile of dishes, the unset table, the musty scent, my mom's empty closet. It was a shock to the sys-tem, and all I could think to do was reach for a snack.

Thankfully for my body, my dad didn't keep much food in the house. Not for dietary reasons, but just because he was a single dude. The only thing we ate was frozen turkey meatballs and brown rice from Trader Joe's. On special occasions, he would bring home a roasted chicken from Gelson's, and we would stand over the counter, eating the whole damn thing with our hands. We didn't talk much the year I lived there. Mostly because he worked a lot, and

I tried to stay out as much as I could, still avoiding full acceptance of my parents' split. Moving back home after being on your own for so long is hard enough, but moving back into a shell of what used to be your family home is downright depressing. Standing in the kitchen, inhaling chicken, was our only real quality time together. Even if we didn't say much, we knew, with each bite, that we loved and supported each other. These are some of my fondest memories of my dad—primitive carnivore memories— and to my surprise, not only did my relationship with my dad grow stronger, but I quickly started to shed the pounds of ice cream and beer I had so easily packed on in college. (If you're going to go on the Glen Schwartz diet, consult a dietician.)

In between the turkey meatballs, I started to pursue my acting career. I remember so clearly meeting with my very first agent. She was a small woman, with an array of hair extensions and a face that clearly wasn't all hers. I stood before her, in my overalls, and I read the audition scene she had given me. Halfway through, she stopped me. My heart immediately dropped. Was I THAT bad? Should I go back to college and find another career? Should I run out and pretend like I was never there? Did I just poop my pants? I took a deep breath and braced myself for the worst.

"You're clearly good at this, but you need to lose weight." I wasn't sure if I was relieved or embarrassed.

"Oh," I said. "Yes, of course; I can do that. I just love my wine. Haha." I always make alcohol jokes during uncomfortable moments (re: half the jokes in this book).

"Maybe just have one glass a night, then," she said with her nose in the air. Come on, I knew this bitch drank a bottle a night. She was blessed with a small frame and no appetite.

"Sure. I can do that. So, do you want to represent me?" I said.

"Yes, but you should try Pilates. I do Pilates every day. Feel my abs!"

Then—I kid you not—she got up from behind her giant agent table, walked over to me, lifted up her shirt, grabbed my hand, and made me touch her abs. I wanted to die, or wanted her to die. Either option would have made that embarrassing situation far better.

"Yes, wow. Pilates. Yeah. Wow. I'll totally give it a try. Thank you."

I started to bolt toward the exit when she stopped me to say:

"Oh, and never wear that again."

"What?"

"Those overalls—don't wear them again."

"Oh, right. Of course. Never again."

That was my harsh introduction to Hollywood, a backhanded win. I'm not sure if I was more upset about her demand for me to lose weight or to throw out my overalls, but that experience set me up for a lifetime of insecurities walking into any interview. Still to this day, I get full-blown audition anxiety. Also, to this day, I resent Pilates. Both will probably never change.

I did book one job through that waistline Nazi, though, and it would change my life and the way I treated my body forever. It was a local play, which in LA isn't regarded very highly compared to places like New York, but at the time it felt like a HUGE deal. It was a drama about homeless kids, and everyone involved seemed so cool. Looking back, I'm pretty sure the director was trying to start some sort of cult, but that's a story for another book. Anyway, he told us on the first day that we all needed to lose weight so we would look more like street kids. My heart started to race; I felt like I was back in the nutritionist office, or at Weight Watchers, or touching my agent's six-pack. I begged my dad to help me pay for a personal trainer to get me in shape for this breakout role. He still reminds me that I have an open tab in need of closing. (Let's see how this book goes, Dad.) For months, I was on a strict work-out regimen and ate like a bunny. I jump roped my brains out and went to the tanning salon fifteen too many times. I was suddenly a stereotypical LA actor, and I felt fuck-ing great. Now, listen, I'm not promoting excessive exer-cise or looking like leather to make you feel good. I don't think being skinny is the formula for making you happy or successful. If anything, I think that constant struggle to try to achieve a certain weight is ultimately harmful and certainly depressing. I do think having a goal, like feel-ing comfortable in just my underwear, in an unnecessary orgy scene, in front of an audience including my grandma, ended up making me feel fantastic. For the first time in forever, I felt sexy, confident, and in control…even if my grandma was mortified.

Not surprisingly, that play didn't do anything for my career, although it's a blessing it didn't end it. I did gain an appreciation for exercise, and that was worth every night of that awkwardly public orgy. Throughout the rest of my twenties, I would wake up every morning, work out hard, make YouTube videos, go on dates, and repeat the next day. I became my own little machine. I was able to eat a healthy amount, drink as much booze as I wanted, and still get up and run the next day. I no longer owned a pair of overalls—I was finally getting the sweet taste of living in the body I had always dreamed of. Little did I realize my thirtieth birthday would wake me from this delightful dream. It was fun while it lasted.

Although now that I read that sentence back as I type, I'm certain hindsight is clouding my memory. I look at pictures from that time, and I looked great, but the reality was I felt bad about myself then too. I have thought and probably always will think I'm overweight because the moment someone puts that into your brain, it sticks with you. Every day, I struggle to stop analyzing every picture or video I see of myself. I still have difficulty getting dressed and feeling confident. It's an exhausting daily hurdle I've been jumping for thirty-five years, which is why I was so elated when I was reunited with my denim security blanket.

Sadly, the pressure to look a certain way is unavoidable,

especially in the entertainment business. If you are even slightly bigger than the models you see in the magazines, you are slapped with a title like "overweight" or "fat," and that's not fair. It's not fair that I get triggered if one lousy kid in the middle of America leaves a comment on my Instagram saying, "She looks old." It's not fair that I can't feel settled unless I go to the gym every day, and even so, I still feel like I could have stayed longer. It's not fair that every woman I've ever met feels like she isn't good enough, pretty enough, skinny enough, or young enough. It's just not fair.

I know I'm supposed to be a role model as a "social media influencer," a godmother, a teacher, and a writer, but I'm at a loss here. I don't have the answer for this one. All I know is that it's a never-ending battle to feel like you're enough and to accept the sentiment that you are "perfect the way you are." Every day since I can remember, I wake up and immediately pull up my shirt and look at myself in the mirror. I assess what I look like and that determines how my day is going to go, and that's fucked up, you guys. Yet, over the years I've slowly come to understand that I'm more than that. Even if I haven't fully implemented that belief, deep down I know it to be true. Why else would we be on this earth? Why else would we be given these specific bodies?

I used to think I was a tall, skinny bitch in my past life, which is why I'm a short, curvy lady in this one. Maybe that's true, but I also think we can learn from the challenges our age and bodies present. What if we accept the fact that we are exactly as we are supposed to be and everything positive that comes to us is a result of that? Would we hate ourselves so much? I mean, if I can attribute all the wonderful opportunities that have come to me because I have simply been me, then how could I not love my body regardless of its size and age? No, you didn't pick up this book from the self-help aisle; you just stumbled across my ongoing mission to try to understand the way our minds work.

I'm now going to make the following promises and hope that you will hold me to them: I will stop looking at my body in the mirror every morning and letting that determine my mood for the day. I will continue to fuel my body with wholesome foods and moderate exercise but will not deprive it of French fries and couch time when it craves it. I will be kind to myself when I see signs of aging and avoid people who like to constantly point them out. I will cheer you on as you find love for your body and keep you laughing on those days that may be a little harder. I will continue to explore how we, together, can make this world a little gentler on all of us.

There is one promise, however, that I will never make—no matter who demands it. I will NEVER stop wearing my overalls, because I feel fucking great in them. And in the end, that's all that really matters.

Fake It Till You Make It, or Until You Panic and Succumb to Zoloft

I'm disturbed, I'm depressed, I'm inadequate. I've got it all!

—George Costanza

For thirty-three years, I avoided asking for help. My mom still reminds me that I would freeze with fear if she needed me to go up to the McDonald's counter to get more ketchup. I couldn't do it, not if it meant having to request something from someone I didn't know. She also frequently apologizes for fueling my body with chicken nuggets. Totally unrelated, but I wanted to let you know, Mom, I forgive you.

Unfortunately, asking for ketchup was just the beginning of the fears I would acquire as time went on. Initially, it would appear that I was just a shy kid, but as the years unfolded, it became more and more apparent that I had a lot more going on than a timid spirit. I was like a rubber band ball, the kind that weird kid in school would make that you were actually kind of jealous of but never patient enough to make on your own. My first few rubber bands began with not wanting to ask fast-food employees for things, followed by faking I didn't have questions for my teachers, wrapped up in avoiding talks with my parents about what's bothering me, succeeded by canceling plans with my friends because I was too sad, then suddenly being thirty and this metaphorical ball becoming so big that the final rubber band snapped, and I was left a broken mess who would panic every time I left the house.

I remember once being at the airport, headed to New York for the Tribeca Film Festival. I was going to screen one of my shows there, and I was extremely honored for the opportunity. I had put so much time and heart into the project, and I felt like I was finally being recognized by someone other than my mom. I thought this had the potential to be a serious stepping-stone in my career. Spoiler alert: It didn't do a damn thing for my career, but that's beside the point.

I was totally fine when I woke up the day of my trip. I felt calm as I got ready and took an Uber to the airport. Yet, the minute I stepped foot into the terminal, my anxiety hit me like a ton of bricks. I was dizzy and nauseous, hot then cold. My heart was racing, my chest felt heavy, and all I wanted to do was go back home.

I can still picture how everything around me looked— as if it were all photoshopped, with the colors hyper-saturated and the edges blurred. Imagine if Van Gogh's *Starry Night* wasn't a sky, but rather, an airport. Everything swirled together. I could hardly see straight. I rushed to the bathroom, ran a paper towel under the cold water, and placed it behind my neck, trying to calm myself. Then I raced through security (TSA PreCheck is great for social anxiety) and headed right to my happy place: the bar. Giving no fucks that it was 7:30 in the morning, I slammed back two mimosas, sans OJ. Who wants extra calories with their morning booze? It's like people who order Diet Cokes with their fast-food meal. Whatever—we're all just doing the best we can.

Immediately, my insides felt warm, and my mind slowed down. The swirled surroundings began to unwind themselves, until everything was back in its proper position. The heightened colors returned to their softer hues, and suddenly I could breathe again. I called my mom, because I'm an adult who sometimes needs her mommy, and began to cry.

"I can't do this. It's not fair. I work too hard to not be able to enjoy it. I don't want to feel like this anymore."

I don't know what she said in response—the champagne and panic hangover clouded my memory—but I'm sure it was something calming and encouraging, because my mother is a saint who knows how to deal with my crazy. I do, however, remember this being one of the times when I realized I needed to ask for help. As much as I appreciate Van Gogh's paintings, I knew I could no longer live in one, or I'd soon be chopping off my own ear.

Enter therapy. I had been in and out of talk therapy throughout my twenties but it never seemed to stick. This was probably due to my unwillingness to do the hard work—it was far easier to complain about everything than to actually do anything about it. I'd announce to my family that I wanted to get help, but then I'd avoid unveiling the uncomfortable issues in my sessions. On top of that, I shuffled through a series of bad therapists, making me weary of the whole process. I once had an older male therapist who couldn't grasp why I had a hard time getting dressed in the morning. I was having daily breakdowns, throwing my clothes all over the place, just trying to find something I felt confident in. His suggestion, through a judgmental smirk, was to pick out the outfit the night before. I don't know if he's never had a woman in his life, but something you think looks good on you one day could look like complete garbage the next. It all depends on what you've eaten the night before, how much sleep you got, the way the fucking wind is blowing, and any other nonsensical thing, but really it was because I was surely experiencing body dysmorphia. I can't believe this dude thought hanging up an outfit the night before was going to fix it all. Must be nice to wear the same lame sweater and slacks every day, you overpriced dummy.

It wasn't until that point in my thirties, when the world would swirl every time I left my house, that I realized I couldn't fake that I was ok anymore. I was beyond ready to do the work I had been putting off up until now. In fact, I knew I didn't have much choice, especially if I wanted a chance at finding a partner to build a life with. I know, thanks to Oprah's SuperSoul Sundays, you have to love yourself before you can even think of letting a partner in.

I also know I felt like a failure because I had heard that your thirties are supposed to be the greatest time of your life, when your confidence is at an ultimate high and your propensity for finding joy is guaranteed. If my current state was the best it was going to get, I was in serious trouble. I wish Oprah would have told me that a magic middle-age fairy doesn't come down and bestow you with self-assurance and clarity once you turn thirty. Maybe then I would have worked a little harder in my twenties. No such luck; I had to get help if I stood a chance of enjoying this age, like everyone else who raves about it does.

I was referred to a therapist through a friend who was even nuttier than me. She seemed to have been making improvements, so I figured I was in decent hands. Not to mention the office was walking distance from my home, giving me very few excuses not to go. Anxious-pro tip: Make mentally hard things as physically easy as possible. If I had the opportunity to use the miserable LA traffic as an out for showing up to a therapy session, I'd NEVER go. No one walks in LA, so foot traffic couldn't be a valid excuse.

I sat across from a middle-aged woman with long, dark hair and a calm energy about her. She asked me why I was there, and I paused.

"How much time you got?"

We both laughed, even though I'm sure she's heard that joke a million times. I was uncomfortable. I wanted to ask for help so badly, but despite the fact that I was sitting in front of the person I was paying to help me, I didn't know how to make myself that vulnerable. Instead, I made jokes the whole session, barely skimming the service of what was really going on with me. Honestly, at that point, I didn't even know what was going on with me, so I definitely couldn't articulate it. After a few sessions, as I grew more secure with the woman in front of me, and my desire to fight my initial resistance grew, I began to find the words to describe what it felt like.

Imagine facing your greatest fear: Standing in front of a giant snake. Staring into the barrel of a gun pointed at you. Drowning in the deepest, darkest ocean. Then envision how your body would react. Heart racing. Head spinning. Stomach churning. Think about the thoughts swirling in your mind. "This is it." "It's all over." "Holy shit." Now take away the catalyst, the justification for these feelings. Replace that snake with an everyday situation like standing in a park. Switch out the barrel of a gun for a crowded mall. Instead of drowning in the ocean, you're walking through a brightly lit grocery store. Can you picture it? The spinning room, the racing thoughts? Can you feel your throat closing, your palms getting clammy? This is what I would feel every time I left the house, went to a job, or simply tried to engage in a situation that I wasn't 100 percent in control of. This is what I explained to her, through whimpered speech, and welled-up eyes.

"It sounds like you have social anxiety. And OCD. And…"

"Ok, that's a solid start. We can just work on those for

the moment," I said, afraid to know what other labels I was going to be slapped with.

The therapist wasn't wrong. In fact, she was starting to see the real me. Finally, someone could identify what I had been trying so hard to cover up for the last thirty years, and it was liberating. It felt great to take off my mask and show her my truth. Sure, it was going to be challenging and dark, but I was ready to unpack it, sit with it, and then change it.

OCD stands for obsessive-compulsive disorder. The obsessive-compulsive part can manifest in many different ways. Most of us probably think of someone washing their hands a million times, or locking and unlocking the door exactly seven times, but compulsions can also live in your thoughts. This is the case for lucky old me. I will think about something that could happen or has happened ad nauseam until I work myself into a full-blown panic attack. Most of the time, the obsession is centered around my health, and it has heightened as I've gotten older. I'm unreasonably concerned that something will suddenly happen to my body, and I will have no control over it. I am in pretty good health, but that doesn't stop my mind from obsessing in the form of what-ifs. Even when I get a cold, I spiral into a series of increasingly dark thoughts.

"What if I never get better?"

"What if this turns into something life threatening?"

"What if there is actually a larger underlying issue that is being overshadowed by this cold, that will eventually reveal itself as something terrible after it's too late to treat because I was busy blowing my nose thinking it was a cold?"

Exhausting, right? You don't want to be inside my brain when I get the flu.

My obsessive thoughts about my health escalate when I'm in public, adding social anxiety to my mental issues cocktail. I always assumed social anxiety meant having trouble socializing at parties or anywhere there are large groups of people. Everyone on the internet seems to throw the term "social anxiety" around in memes about being antisocial, and yes, that's certainly part of it. The root of it, though, at least for me, is thinking something bad is going to happen to me while I'm in public. I have this unjustifiable fear of passing out while I'm at the mall or anywhere there are large crowds. Please note: I've never passed out, not once in my life. So, this all sounds beyond ridiculous but feels so plausible in the moment. The concern is amplified any time I'm by myself, and even if I can talk myself off the mental ledge, my body still flares into the uncontrollable panic symptoms.

I've worked tirelessly with my therapist to try to get to the root of where these fears come from, because that's the only way to even begin to move past them. Personally, I prefer the "sweeping old shit under the rug" method, but after thirty years of doing that, the rug has come unraveled.

We concluded that my obsessive worries about my health stem from my childhood. This isn't groundbreaking—most issues come from your formative years—but my therapist helped me pinpoint the major moments that got me to this place and the missed opportunities when I could have asked for help.

I dealt with a lot of death growing up, from family members who had grown ill to friends my age who were taken too soon. I remember the initial shock, the endless crying, and the sterile funerals. Those things are all so crystal clear. What I don't have is any memory of the conversations my parents would have with me about these losses. Not a fault of my memory, I'm afraid. Rather, I think, a result of my parents' resistance to having those hard conversations. They were adamant about hiding most things from my brother and me. I know they were trying to protect us, but that emotional sanitization ultimately led to some deep-rooted issues I'm still trying to sort out. This avoidance is culturally very Jewish. Don't talk about your feelings, don't talk about uncomfortable situations, and don't even try to talk out a problem with another family member. Just hold it all in. Push it all down. Move on. The only exception to the rule: You can talk shit about other people. Especially the Rosenblatts at the end of the street. "Did you see the new car Mr. Rosenblatt drove home in?" "I thought he got fired from his job at the bank." "Seems like a terrible financial move to me." "Maybe it's a midlife crisis." "Did you see Mrs. Rosenblatt at the deli last night?" "Talk about crisis—looks like someone's been spending time at the plastic surgeon." "Think she's having an affair?" This was my first introduction to reality TV.

Anyhow, due to the avoided conversations, the big ones being sickness and death, I assumed dying was something that happened suddenly and traumatically. I figured it was just a flip of the switch, and then you were dead. In the fourth grade, I had my head in my English workbook, when the telephone in the classroom rang. After a brief conversation, my teacher hung up and told me I needed to pack up my stuff and head to the office. I put my Lisa Frank binder into my backpack and beelined out the door. I was surprised to be greeted by my mom and dad. It was the middle of the day—why were they there? They both have full-time jobs; this couldn't be good. A moment later my brother came walking through the door, with his backpack full, clearly having gotten the same call. We all loaded into the car as my dad said they needed to tell us something but wanted to wait until we got home. We all sat in silence, the whole way. Talk about a thrill ride. My mind raced, trying to guess what this could possibly be about. Maybe they were going to tell us we were moving, or they were getting a divorce, or we were in trouble for playing around with mom's expensive lipsticks. My brother and I had an affinity for dressing up in costumes and putting on full faces of makeup. He looked fantastic in a blue shadow and a pink lip—how he didn't turn out to be a drag queen is beyond me. When we got home, we all sat on the couch, formally, as if we were in some sort of group therapy. My heart was beating out of my chest.

"Your aunt died," Dad said as the tears welled up in

his eyes. This is one of the only times I've ever seen my dad cry.

"Auntie Arlene?" My brother asked, and we wailed in unison. She was the only aunt we had—of course it was her. He just had to ask, to properly digest this crushing information.

"Yes," my dad said, processing the fact that his sister was now gone.

We all sat there, not saying anything, just crying, for what felt like forever. We had lost a core member of our small family, and in that moment, I learned what real loss felt like. Here's the thing, though: In my fourth-grade brain, she was alive one day and then suddenly dead the next. No one explained to me what had happened to her. My family didn't provide any context for this loss. We don't talk about things, remember? I just assumed that's how life and death worked—in one day, out the next. It wasn't until this past year, on Mother's Day, when my cousin explained to me what had actually happened to her mother. I was shocked to find out she had been very sick in the hospital for several days prior to her passing. This wasn't the sudden "flip of the switch" I had believed all these years.

After that major loss, a string of random and sudden ones flooded my world. My best friend, at fifteen, was struck by a car. She died on the spot, with her dad watching. Within a year, another young girl I knew was out riding her bike when she was hit by a car. She died on the spot, with her family watching. A year later, my grandma was complaining of a headache, and then she just died. On the spot, with my grandpa watching. Common theme here? Besides complete gut-wrenching tragedies? Every death I knew about happened within seconds. This is when you guys check the description of the book again to see if you somehow misread "comedy" for "depression-inducing drama."

The point of all this is I didn't have a handle on sickness or death, even though I've dealt with so much of it. All I gained in those years of mourning was obsessive health and social anxiety, wondering when it would be my turn. If we had talked about these things as a family, or if I had reached out for help, I wonder if I would be dealing with my often very debilitating issues.

I worked with my therapist for almost three years, not missing a week, determined to break through whatever blocks were keeping me from getting better. It wasn't easy; I spent most of my sessions blowing through boxes of tissues and wanting to quit. She was patient, taking me slowly through talk therapy—methodically picking apart my past and connecting it to my present. Together, we came up with a set of tools I could use when my anxiety flared up. I got pretty good at self-talk and downloaded a meditation app on my phone to calm me when I couldn't do it myself. There would be months when I would feel like it was all working, when I could go to the mall and everything wouldn't be spinning. Then, I'd have a setback, causing me to bury myself in my comfort zone. I'd avoid leaving the house, because I was too exhausted to even attempt to quiet my fears.

At one point, after a couple of years of us working together, my therapist suggested I go on medication. In her opinion, we had made so much progress, but there appeared to be some chemical imbalances that we simply couldn't fix with talk alone. If you think my neurotic brain took that suggestion well, I haven't done a great job explaining how it works.

One of my most delightful neuroses is being frightened of taking medication. I'll even avoid Advil if I can because I am convinced it does more harm than good. I told her I wasn't ready to take that route, even if I was still suffering. Instead I decided I would try anything to avoid turning to medication. I downward dogged, I meditated, I tried acupuncture. I swallowed herbs, I journaled, I exercised. I upped my therapy sessions to twice a week, smoked medical marijuana, cut out caffeine. I even spent more money on crystals than I am willing to admit, but nothing ever fully worked. (I know, shocking—the crystals didn't cure me.)

On November 8, 2016, I finally decided I had no choice but to ask for medication. It was the day of the election. In my mind, I believed we were about to elect Hillary Clinton as our forty-fifth president (I miss those naïve days). I was full of emotions as I headed to the polling place on what was slated to be an incredible historic day. Due to the anticipated large turnout of voters, they moved my polling spot from its usual location at the old folks' home down the street, to the local park's very large rec room. When I pulled up, circling the block several times because parking was impossible, my heart started to race. I noticed a huge line of people out the door and suddenly felt like I was on a rocking boat. Normally, I would have just turned around and gone home, avoiding the stress altogether. However, this was not an option for me in that moment. I was not willing to miss out on voting for our first female president. This was more important, as a woman, a godmother, an American, than any anxiety I would have to deal with.

With a flushed face, I made my way to the line. The more time I spent waiting, the more my surroundings began to swirl. Just like that time in the airport, all my senses were heightening to uncomfortable levels. The sounds of children playing in the park grew unbearably loud, the smell of coffee from the woman behind me flooded my nostrils, the sweat on my palms felt like puddles, and my heart seemed to be pumping faster than it ever had. I quickly moved my heels up and down, trying to distract my body from feeling anything else.

When I finally got into the polling room, I was near the point of passing out. At this stage, not only was I fighting the battle of being alone in a public place with a ton of people, but I was also feeding off an extremely heightened emotional environment. The energy, stress, and excitement from everyone around me was palpable. I felt like I was being electronically hooked up to every single person in that room and I was about to short-circuit.

When I stepped up to the voting booth, I could hardly see straight. I thought to myself, "I have to leave. I can't do this." I started to tear up, realizing my anxiety was going to ruin my life. If I couldn't punch that ballot and contribute to one of the most important days I'd live to see, I would forever be devastated. Sadly, regardless of the fact that I forced myself to stay and contribute my vote, the result of the election still left me devastated.

I started a small dose of Zoloft not long after that day. I would be lying if I said it was a smooth transition. I had many days when I felt even worse than I did before I took it. I was lucky to have a friend who was also transitioning onto a similar drug, so we would check in with each other regularly, assuring the other that the experiences were mutual and "normal." Finally, after about a month and a half, I balanced out and started feeling like myself again. Only now, I was a less anxious and far more grounded version of myself. For the first time, in a long time, I finally felt like me, and it was fantastic.

This isn't an ad for Zoloft, or even a push for medication. Everybody's body chemistry is different and should be handled individually with the help of a medical professional. It's just a look back at what I was willing to put myself through, for so many years, because I didn't want to ask for help. I suffered throughout my twenties, faking like I was doing great, because I wanted to look good to everyone around me. You know what turned out not to be a good look? Suffering all those years behind closed doors.

Now, as a thirty-five-year-old woman, I am able to let go of faking perfection and finally take some ownership over my life and my mental health. I'm not claiming that I am 100 percent healed, but the good days far outweigh the bad. I still go to therapy to find new tools to keep my symptoms at bay, and continue to examine where all of this stems from. Even though it seems shitty at first, the more I confront the past, the lighter I feel in the present.

At least mentally.

I don't read the side effects on drug bottles, because the minute I do, I suddenly have every symptom listed. I did still come to find out Zoloft causes weight gain. Didn't have to read about it though—my tight pants said it all. But the ill-fitting denim is worth it, because now I can enjoy my life and even have fun out in public. I still get nervous at airports or really any time I'm in a large crowd. Only now, my body doesn't kick into panic overdrive, and my former physical reactions to the fear hardly ever flare. I also don't obsess over a thought or go down the rabbit hole of what ifs every time I get sick. Now I'm more capable of living in the present and taking everything one moment at a time. I've pledged to be honest with my feelings and ask for help without judging myself for doing so. (I hope I've inspired you to do the same.)

I think it's safe to say I understand why people declare the thirties are so great. I don't think it's fair to attribute the grandness to the actual age, for I've learned that everyone moves at their own pace, and a number can't dictate that. But if you're willing to take pride in your mental health and put in the time and necessary measures it takes to sort through your "stuff," then you will be gifted with the space to experience all the positive things the world around you has to offer.

Despite the amount of Zoloft I'm on, I'll still never be able to ask for ketchup, or anything for that matter, at McDonald's. Not due to my fear of asking, but simply because I'm terrified of putting that stuff in my body. My mom already did enough damage to me with the nuggets. Thanks, Mom!

Baby Names vs. Binge Eating

You want a beautiful name? Soda.

—George Costanza

My mom wanted to name me Eve. Sure, it's a great name, and I bet it serves many women well. But you guys, my brother's name is Adam. When he was two years old, my mom was pregnant with me and thought, "Hey! How cute would it be to have a son named Adam and a daughter named Eve!" I'm not sure if we can blame the "pregnancy brain" for this one, or pure insanity, but my brother and I came dangerously close to bearing names that would have gotten us beaten the fuck up. Or, at the very least, would have cursed our relationship with incestuous undertones. Thank god, my dad campaigned for Lisa, or this could have ended badly.

Names are a weird thing. They seem so simple, but that one word (or two, if you're from the South and/or have a parent who can't make decisions) can define a person for the rest of their life. Whether it's accurate or not, specific names have specific associations. In the eighties, if your name was Tiffany or Heather, you were a hot bitch. If your name was Kathy or Andrea, you were an ugly nerd. Maybe it was TV and film that brought us these stereotypes, but they were usually spot-on. Have you ever met someone, and after hearing their name you think, "Yeah, they do look like a [fill in the name]"? It happens to me all the time. Although, every once in a while, I'll meet someone who is the polar opposite of their name. I'm always taken aback when that happens, then ultimately in awe of them for defying the path their parents unintentionally set out for them. Good on you, Sandra, for not being a doctor's office front-desk receptionist who loves her Diet Cokes and acrylic nails.

In seventh grade, I started at a new school. It was one of those schools that went from pre-k to twelfth grade, but because most other elementary schools ended after sixth grade, there was a flood of new students the year I started. It was great knowing I wasn't going to be the only new kid—I could blend right in. The goal was to come in, assess the social situation, and then plan my attack. Sadly, this wasn't an option for every new student.

First day of history class, Ms. Bernstein walks into the room. She was probably in her late fifties, but in my memory, she was as ancient as a dinosaur. This poor woman had a reputation for being a witch who spray-painted her head to make her thinning hair appear fuller. It didn't work. It just made her head look like a preschool art project. God bless her, kids are mean. The first thing she did was pull out her roster to take attendance. I always hated that part of class: Even though all you had to say was "here," it made me so nervous. For that split second, the attention would all be on me. What if I said "here" strangely, or too loud, or too soft, or with a crack in my voice? What if the cute boy in the row ahead of me turned around? Or worse, what if he didn't turn around at all? Is my voice that gross? Is my name that lame? This is how my seventh-grade brain worked. Not much has changed.

Ms. Bernstein began to run down the list. Everyone was in attendance so far, because it was the first day of school. No one tended to mess that one up, but she went through the motions anyway. She was into the *b*'s, when she stopped for a second. We had a fairly diverse student body, so some of the names may have been hard to pronounce at first glance. I assumed she was working the name out in her head. After a beat, with complete confidence, she called out, "RA-GINA HILL." As in, rhymes with Vagina Hill. Everyone busted out in laughter. So much so that Ms. Bernstein had to repeat it. This time, louder.

"RA-GINA HILL?" she practically shouted.

Then a meek voice from the back of the room broke through the laughter and mumbled.

"Um...it's Regina [obviously pronounced: RUH-JEE-NUH]," she said with equal parts embarrassment and pure defeat.

In that one short moment, with that one mispronunci-ation, Regina Hill's high school destiny was set. She was fucked. Ms. Bernstein royally fucked her. She would forever be RA-GINA and have zero chance at hanging with the cool kids.

A few thoughts about this RA-GINA situation...

One: It's so sad that that's how the middle school social game works. I'm sure Regina is doing amazing things now and is totally awesome.

Two: I can't imagine how Ms. Bernstein managed it. Setting aside the fact that Regina is a fairly known name, common sense should have told her that it probably didn't rhyme with the female genitalia. Maybe it was Ms. Bernstein's way of getting back at all the students who had spread rumors and made mean comments about her for centuries. Regina was our innocent scapegoat.

Three: Did Mr. and Mrs. Hill think twice about the fact that the name Regina could possibly be pronounced RA-GINA? Did they look at it and think, "Oh shit, that name kind of looks like 'vagina.' Maybe we should name our daughter something else just in case her senile seventh-grade history teacher mispronounces her name on the first day at her new school and ruins her chance of ever getting laid." I'm hoping they didn't. That would be cruel if they did and proceeded anyway. I'm guessing they thought it was a nice tribute to a great-grandmother. I wonder if that grandmother ever got called RA-GINA by accident. I'd love to watch a documentary about this.

I think Regina would agree that your given name can really dictate your life narrative. There have been so many times when I've been on a dating app and have come across multiple guys with girls' names. No matter how cute they are, I can't do it. I can't date a guy named Lindsey, or Ashley, or Dana. I'm sorry; I can't. Maybe that makes me a shallow bitch, but a shallow bitch who doesn't have to call her lover by a woman's name. Why did their parents do this to them? Was it because they wanted a girl? Did they only decide on female names, and when they found out it wasn't a girl, they were either too dejected or too lazy to choose a boy name? Were they rebelling against the penis? Were they in pure denial? I just don't get it. Same goes for women with guys' names. It's a mindfuck for everyone involved. I'm progressive and support gender neutrality and shit, but let your kid make that decision. Don't make life harder for them. Watch, I'm going to meet the love of my life and his name is going to be Elizabeth.

Needless to say, I am a huge advocate of mindful and thorough planning when it comes to choosing a name for your child. I am not, however, in favor of picking out said name for a child that hasn't even been jizzed into your body yet. I'm sorry—that was over the top and disgusting, but so is naming the theoretical child you are planning to have with your hypothetical husband. Believe me, this is a thing that people really do, and I absolutely cannot handle the absurdity of it.

For the past ten years, around Christmastime, a group of my girlfriends from childhood and I pick a night to throw a "Friends-mas." In truth, we literally never call it that and I'm not sure why I felt the need to give it a cute name. We just send out a group text to pick a time and place to meet. Adorable moniker or not, I always look forward to this night. It's an opportunity to let loose and celebrate, without all the stress that the holidays usually bring (i.e., family).

Right around the time I turned thirty, those holiday nights out began turning into early nights in. Which, listen—I'm into. I'm a total homebody, but I'm also a sucker for tradition. Something about getting dressed up with my friends and spending the night out made me feel young and alive. Wow, that sounds depressing. Point is, I liked our annual night out, but I had made peace with our revised tradition. Just as I finally did, I got hit with another curveball. One of our friends in the holiday circle got knocked up, with twins. By the way, that's my actual nightmare. Not only are you pregnant, but you now have two little aliens growing inside of you. I guess the only redemption there is you can technically say you're eating for three, which is literally what I did when I realized my friendships were never going to be the same.

Welcome to Friends-mas 3.0, my least favorite version, filled with nothing but baby talk. I love my friends more than anything, and I want them to have as many babies as their uteruses desire, but selfishly I wasn't ready for our annual celebration to turn into discussions about burp cloths and birthing plans. I didn't want to embrace this huge change. Why did everything have to suddenly be different? Friends-mas 3.0 made me hate Christmas, my endless appetite, and most of all, baby names.

Due to the nixing of bars as our holiday setting, we were

limited in our location options. It was either my bachelorette pad or my lawyer friend's gorgeous condo. We didn't even need to flip a coin. My Uber pulled up to her condo, and I unloaded the bags of snacks I had brought as a thank-you for not having to host myself. Also, as reassurance that there would be enough munchies to keep me in the holiday spirit. I've been to one too many parties where there has been only one measly bowl of potato chips. Get out of my face with that lack of effort. Maybe it's the Jewish grandma in me or the former fat kid, but if you're having guests, you should always have enough food to feed an army. Extra points if hot Army men actually attend. I'm still waiting for that day, but I'm prepped and ready if it should ever happen.

As I shut the car door, I flashed a peace sign and told the driver I was going to give him five stars. That was a total lie—he was only getting three from me. That dude drove so slowly, and his car smelled like a gallon of Lysol had spilled in the trunk. I assumed it was on purpose to cover up the smell of the dead body. (I'd been on a true-crime podcast kick.) I looked up at the perfectly land-scaped building, took a deep breath, and headed inside. I was ready to dominate this house party.

The door swung open, and I was greeted by the lovely hostess, who was dressed in expensive sweatpants. I can't even imagine the day when I can justify owning sweatpants that don't have seventeen years of history in them. Most of my sweats have been with me since college. They were on me through every breakup and breakdown. I'm not even joking when I say that I am currently wearing a pair of sweats I got in 2001. The elastic in the waistband is no longer intact, so I have to hold them up when I'm walking the dog down the street. I'm fairly certain my neighbors have seen my ass crack more than a few times. Even so, I'm still not inclined to buy new ones—perhaps that's something I should discuss in therapy.

I guess I missed the memo about the dress code. I just assumed a holiday party meant whipping out Spanx and sucking into sparkles. I hadn't taken into account that we were in the third iteration of this holiday tradition. Apparently, we'd now given up and were celebrating in sweatpants on the couch, throwing filters on our pictures so we could avoid wearing makeup. I had never wanted to rip off my fake eyelashes to fit in more than I did in that moment. I didn't have time though, because I was promptly asked to take off my shoes, so I dismounted from my three-inch heels and headed into the party with my nice pants dragging on the floor and my overly flashy eyelashes.

My friends were all gathered on the oversized L-shaped couch. One of those gorgeous ones you see in all the design magazines that you wish you could afford, let alone have space for. The room smelled of rich candles and fresh flowers. Jazz standards hummed under the chatter of the ladies, and the room was bright from the newly installed recessed lighting. Unless you've seen orchids at a dive bar, I was pretty certain we were light-years away from how things used to be.

After greeting the crew, I headed to the kitchen to seek out the booze situation.

"What are you guys having to drink?" I asked, as I opened the fridge to find nothing more than bottled water.

"I'm not drinking; we're trying to get pregnant," one friend said, with pure hope in her eyes.

"I'm not drinking either. I'm trying to slim down for the wedding," another friend said, while taking tiny bites from a dry rice cracker.

"No drinking for me—I'm on a cleanse," another friend said quietly, cowering as far from the granite-topped kitchen island full of food as she could get.

The last friend didn't need to say anything, her twin-bearing belly saying it all.

"Party time!" I declared, probably a bit too snidely. I grabbed a bottle of water and a whole bag of tortilla chips. I have portion-control issues, and this was going to be a long night.

The conversations that night were indeed mostly about babies. We all sat around the pregnant belly, genuinely excited about the pending arrivals. Even me. Although I resented the universe for presenting me with all this baby shit considering I'm not even close to thinking about having one, it was fun to imagine one of my dearest friends having little mini versions of herself. She is just the sweetest person, so her having babies meant more sweet humans were on the way. We obviously need more people like that in this world. Not reason enough for me to want to have one myself, but I was thrilled knowing she was taking one (or in this case, two) for the team.

The night was actually going pretty well, all baby talk considered. I was enjoying the conversations, embracing the new topics, and feeling hopeful that our friendship was evolving into a beautiful new chapter. Then it happened. One question, and the night was steered into pure hell for me. One question, and I was catapulted into a full-blown emotional free fall. Seven words, pure insanity.

"What are you going to name them?" someone—I can't even remember who—asked.

"Oh, we're not sure yet. We have a whole list though. Do you wanna see it?" she asked as she pulled out her phone.

I know what you're thinking: "What's the big deal? She's pregnant with twins. She should be thinking about names." Correct. I said it myself. Naming your child is a very important decision. What came next, however, was beyond my comprehension.

This excited expecting mother started going down the list, reciting names she and her husband had been considering. Each one was followed by an "ooh" and an "aah" from everyone in the room. When she got to a particularly popular name, thanks to celebrities making them so, someone would immediately shout, "Oh, that's on my list too!"

"Me too!" another friend would chime in.

"We also really love the name Stella," said the only actual pregnant person there.

There was an audible gasp from the group. Apparently,

everyone wanted a "Stella." Not just in theory, but also in an actual thought-out, written-down kind of way. As soon as the Stella floodgates were opened, everyone pulled out their cell phones and started comparing dream names. This is not a joke. This was a real-life thing that real-life people did because they have real-life baby names picked out before they have a real-life baby inside them. What the actual fuck?

Everyone continued to scroll through their lists, taking turns to mention some of their favorite curated names. I wasn't sure at this point if they were excitingly comparing or aggressively competing. If two people had the same name on a list, it seemed to get a little tense. I watched, imagining their brains at work, doing the math, considering their ovulation calendars, plotting out how quickly they could get knocked up so as to be the first one to pop out a "Ryder." What kind of name is that, anyway? Is that even a name? No time for questions. Must. Claim. Name. First.

"Do you have a list?" one of my friends asked, with what felt like a tinge of accusation.

Mind you, I had JUST broken up with my boyfriend, in a rather dramatic ending. Even if I did have a list of names, the thought of which makes me want to barf, there is no way in hell this conversation would be healthy to my psyche.

"Nope," I said, as I stood up to get another snack. I considered walking past the kitchen and straight out the front door to the nearest roof I could jump off. I didn't want to be there. In fact, I had no business being there. I had nothing to contribute to the conversation. I was thirty-two, single, and had named my dog Unicorn. I was literally not qualified for this night.

I don't think anyone noticed I was upset, or even absent from the rest of the discussion. I pretended to have trouble with the trash compactor and then with the ice maker to avoid going back into the mind-numbing conversation. As I mimicked futzing with all the appliances, I couldn't help but examine my friendships. Those amazing women in the other room had been the most stable relationships in my life for more than fifteen years. Why did I suddenly feel like they had all grabbed a piece of the rug and simultaneously ripped it out from under me with one big "Stella/Ryder" swoop? Why did they all seem overjoyed to be having a conversation that I had absolutely no connection to? Had I outgrown these relationships? Or worse, had they outgrown me? More immediately, how was I going to get out of this situation without causing a scene or revealing my flooding emotions? I didn't have the answers. So, I inhaled a second bag of chips followed by a slice of cake, then another, and, I'm ashamed to say, then another. I don't even like cake.

Let's talk about coping mechanisms. In this case, a fancier way of saying binge eating. I am aware that what I did that night isn't healthy. In fact, I'm pretty lucky I didn't shit my pants right then and there. I usually have some self-control, but that night I purposely pushed past it. I forcefully took down more cake than a five-foot-one person should ever take down, in order to escape the reality that everything around me was changing. Could I have pulled a friend aside and expressed how I was feeling without them judging me? Absolutely. Could I have excused myself and called my therapist to ask for help? One hundred percent. Could I have limited my food intake, faked interest for the night, and sorted out my emotions when I got home? In theory. But my intentions to eat my sorrows were strong, and I did just that.

The night ended early, with exchanges of gifts and well wishes for the rest of the holiday season. I don't remember what I got or whom I said what to; I just know I was thrilled to finally get to leave. I randomly had the same Uber driver on the way home. I prayed he hadn't seen my previous rating. I was quiet the whole car ride, which isn't my usual MO. I have a tendency to overengage with the drivers. I figure if I'm super nice and chatty with them, they won't kill me. (I should really lay off the crime podcasts.) I just stared out the window, replaying the whole night, hoping I wouldn't puke sprinkles before I got home.

The next morning, I woke up with an awful stomachache and a heavy heart. I lay staring at the ceiling, evaluating the choices I had made. Not just the night before, but throughout my life. Dramatic, I know. Though this isn't uncommon behavior for a self-deprecating overthinker. I wonder if the name Lisa lends itself to that description. Damn it, maybe Eve would have been better after all. Anyway, lying in bed, I couldn't stop obsessing over the fact that I felt so alienated from my friends. Why was I so far behind? Why did I care so much that my friends had these name lists on their phones and I didn't? Why couldn't I get a handle on my emotions in the moment? My brain ran circles around itself, while my stomach ran me to the toilet. Don't binge eat cake, kids. It's not worth it.

My therapist constantly reminds me that I'm too hard on myself. Which ironically makes her seem too tough on me. That's what I'm paying for, I guess. Together we decided that I have a tendency to get so caught up comparing myself to others that it keeps me from living in the moment and enjoying it. What's worse, I judge myself for doing so, making it impossible to cut through the negative self-talk and unhealthy coping habits in order to clearly analyze and grow from the situation. Her suggestion, moving forward, was to take that judgment and turn it into curiosity. Instead of being upset with myself for being so angry about how I reacted to a baby name list, I ought to choose to be curious as to why I got so agitated in the first place. This is a far kinder and more productive way of handling emotions. Easier said than done, I know, but after that night, I hold the word "curious" close to my heart. In fact, if I did have a baby name list, I'd have "Curious" on it. Yet another reason why I'm not ready to have a kid.

That was the last year we had a proper Friends-mas. Not for any particular reason. It's just that everyone got busy with their new babies and families. The older you get, the harder it seems to get everyone in the same place at the same time. I, obviously, still don't have a baby, or a list of baby names. Although, I would be lying if I said I haven't thought about it. Not about making an actual list. After all my ranting, I couldn't possibly allow myself to do that. I have thought, in passing, about names that wouldn't set a kid up for failure. I'm not going to tell you the names; I can't have you stealing them. I know how this game goes. I can, however, share a few I am 100 percent certain I will never choose. Feel free to take them for yourself. Just do me a favor and don't whip your list out at a party. There may be a friend there whose emotions can't handle it—even though she shouldn't be ashamed of where she is in her life, because we are all on our own individual journeys, dictated by fate, set up the minute we are given our very own name.

So now, without further ado, my non-name list:

- Stella
- Ryder
- Regina
- Adam
- Eve
- Lindsey for a boy
- Ashley for a boy
- Dana for a boy

and...

- Ms. Bernstein—although I would consider naming my next dog that. Seriously.

My Gay Boyfriend

Not that there's anything wrong with that!
—Jerry Seinfeld

Writing about breakups feels like such a cliché thing to do, considering I have read endless articles, seen countless movies, and devoured innumerable podcasts that have covered the subject ad nauseam. Yet, each one has struck a chord with me, providing a valuable takeaway or at least a sense of relief knowing I am not alone. So, at the risk of lacking an original thought, I'd love to pass along what I've learned about breakups. After all, I don't believe there is anything commonplace about providing comfort to others through shared experiences. Even the shitty ones. Hot damn, I just talked myself into being your new breakup coach. Let's chat heartbreak.

Things I learned about breakups in my twenties:

- They hurt like a bitch, even if you were the bitch.
- Getting dumped is just as hard as dumping someone.

- Rebound sex is ok, but eating your feelings is way more fun.
- It gets better.

Things I'm learning about breakups in my thirties:

- They still hurt like a bitch, but now they come with an added bonus of the dread of knowing you're that much further from catching up with all your married friends.
- Getting dumped because you're not "the one" is just as hard as realizing you may never find "the one."
- Rebound sex requires too much effort and a thirty-year-old metabolism can't handle copious amounts of pizza.
- It gets better. I think?

There is a footnote to this, or rather the "special case" version that lands somewhere between these two lists. This rarity is reserved for those who have been dumped in their thirties from a relationship that began in their twenties. In one fell swoop, you are tossed back into single life, only this time in a thirty-year-old body (not in shape to impress a new mate), a thirty-year-old brain (not willing to accept that marriage is no longer right around the corner), and a thirty-year-old set of social skills (not an actual thing because you've been sitting around in sweats on the couch for years with the man you thought was going to be yours forever).

I was lucky enough to have been one of the "chosen ones," part of that select group of people who were thrown into their thirties as a newly single individual, with no idea how to start over. I had to start from the ground up—dating apps weren't very popular when I was in my twenties! This was a whole new language I needed to learn, and I'm TERRIBLE at languages. I took Latin in high school specifically because you didn't have to speak it out loud. I STILL barely passed the class.

I am going to stand by the fact that I was lucky to go through this. As shitty as the recovery was, I would never take back the relationship that shaped me into the person I am today. It's my original "Internet Dating" story far before that term was commonly used. A journey of love that turned into the most public online experience one could ever imagine. Literally, for four years, millions of people watched our relationship grow and blossom and eventually fall apart, as the man I wanted to marry came out of the closet and left me to make sense of it all. This sounds like a reality TV show I would binge watch for hours, but honestly, I don't even think the brilliant *Bachelor* producers could come up with something like this. This is my story, my real-life reality show, and I'm finally ready to really talk about it.

The year was 2009. The first African-American president was sworn into office. The swine flu was deemed a global pandemic. The world lost the legendary Michael Jackson. And I met the man who would change my life forever.

I just didn't know it at the time, because he was kind of stinky and acted super weird around me. Meet Shane Dawson. My future ex-boyfriend, who also likes boys.

We met on the set of a television pilot for Comedy Central produced by the Fine Brothers, two of the pioneers of YouTube comedy. I was secretly shitting my pants because I was new to the business and didn't feel like I deserved to be there. I remember sitting in the greenroom with Shane, an innocent-faced young man with perfectly manicured hair, not saying much. I would later learn he was also freaking out because not only was this one of his first professional jobs, but he thought I was "the prettiest girl in the whole world." He used to tell me that all the time. Seriously, the start of our relationship was like the cheesiest Hallmark movie. Apparently, he was stressing out, thinking that I might notice the full Spanx-like bodysuit he was wearing under his costume. He had recently lost more than one hundred pounds, but his skin was still playing catch-up. God bless Jenny Craig and shapewear! I didn't notice because I was too busy getting lost in my own head. This was pre-Zoloft days when going to work instantly fueled my fear that I would do something wrong and ruin my entire career. As if missing one line or messing up my entrance into a scene would put me on a "black list" in Hollywood for the rest of my life. Anxiety defies logic; it's actually pretty impressive.

We sat in silence for a while until an unnaturally tan, overly fit, and alarmingly loud dude tornadoed into the room and stood before us. Without a breath and at the top of his lungs, he introduced himself as our other cast mate, then exited with a manic whirl, not giving us a moment to say anything back. Shane and I finally made eye contact (if you consider mutually weirded out, wide-eyed looks contact), and he cracked a joke about Casting finding that dude on Craigslist. (There's nowhere less trustworthy to find an actor, or anyone, for that matter. Have you read the misconnections section?) We both busted out in uncontrollable laughter. Such a simple joke, but it had us in tears and it was ultimately the catalyst for our relationship. Little did Shane know, I had also gotten hired off of Craigslist. I never told him.

After that shoot, the Fine Brothers introduced me to the world of YouTube. At the time, I barely had a working computer, let alone any idea of what YouTube was. I just assumed it was where cat videos lived. The Fine Brothers graciously opened my eyes to this new platform that allowed creators to produce content, work with like-minded people, and control their own careers. I remember spending hours in their tiny apartment, laughing hysterically as we made silly sketches that would later get millions of views. YouTube was a lot purer back then (she says, before describing her walks uphill to school in the snow and how she often yells at kids to get off her lawn). Truly, the community was so kind and collaborative. Everyone was doing it because it was fun and it fueled their souls and no one was making millions of dollars or filming mindlessly in Suicide Forest. If you aren't familiar with the current YouTube culture, just Google that. It's as horrifying as it sounds.

Shane's name came up a lot while I was working with the Fine Brothers. I learned he had his own channel and was known as the "King of YouTube." With millions of subscribers, he was at the top of his game. Hell, he created the game. The best part was he had done it all on his own. One day, the Fine Bros put him in a sketch with me, and we got to know each other better as we giggled our way through the entire video shoot. I was in awe that this shy kid with a solid Craigslist joke was captivating the hearts of millions of people all over the world. And yet, the more I worked with him, the more I understood why. Shane is universally relatable. He has an undeniable energy that makes anyone he talks to feel like they are understood and cared for. He is pure magic. You can't learn this in an acting class, folks, or buy it at Target, where you can buy pretty much everything. I'll go into that store for toilet paper and come out with a cart full of nonsense that I "totally need." Why I thought I "needed" a tuxedo onesie is beyond me. Please note: Even in a frivolous shopping binge, I have never been able to justify sexy pajamas or lingerie. But tuxedo footie pajamas...absolutely!

People always ask if I knew Shane liked boys. For the record, he identifies as bisexual—"My Gay Boyfriend" was just a better chapter title (he thought so too). To be honest, yes, I did kind of know. I always had a feeling he was at least bi-curious. On our first date, which I initiated via email (DMs didn't exist yet; otherwise, I would have slid right in), I noticed Shane would follow men with his eyes as they passed our table. He didn't do this to women, just men. This continued for a while, until I finally had to say something. When I asked him about it, he told me it was because he's always looking at other men to see how his body compares to theirs. Like I mentioned earlier, he had lost a ton of weight, but he was still very insecure about his physical appearance. So, I believed him. Yet deep down I knew there might have been a little more to it, but I ignored my instincts. After all, I was infatuated with one of the most fascinating people I had ever met, and he was just as excited to hang out with me. Why would I question anything beyond that?

My denial didn't stop other people in my life from constantly poking around once we became "official." I remember Shane sitting next to me while I was on the phone telling a friend that he and I were together. She responded with the same unnerving question everyone else did. Like a record player on loop, I quickly replied with my canned answer: "No. No. We are so happy."

After I hung up, he told me he'd heard her ask if he was gay. He was so embarrassed and told me he was worried about meeting her. Thinking about it now, it hurts my heart. He was already suppressing so many feelings and curiosities. Hearing someone doubt the image he was trying so hard to project must have been heartbreaking.

Eventually, after all the initial questioning and reassuring, we were finally given the space to let our relationship blossom. My favorite memories of Shane happened during this time. The late-night hangouts, the endless laughter, and the viewings of hours upon hours of stupid YouTube videos. I felt like I was a kid again.

Shane often compared himself to Michael Jackson (minus the alleged inappropriate behavior and one-glove look), identifying with the superstar's childlike approach to life. Shane had a pretty rough childhood himself, coming from a poor and abusive household. He was forced to grow up fast and provide for his family. When he became successful, he was able to revert back to some of the childish experiences he had missed out on. We often found ourselves in candy stores and arcades; he preferred soda over booze and had very little to no experience with dating. For the first few months, Shane brought me flowers every single time he came to see me. He genuinely thought that was what boyfriends were "supposed" to do. I never corrected him; I love flowers. More so, I loved his innocence—which sounds creepy, I know. Especially considering that I also took his virginity. Did I mention I am five years older than he is? I swear I'm not a supercougar weirdo. My point is Shane and I had a magical partnership that was filled with firsts, childlike wonder, belly laughs, and eight million people watching our every move. This is not an exaggeration.

I love reality TV. In fact, I believe I may mention it more often than my family in this book. That's the kind of sick love I have for it. Even after a show is over, I like to stalk all the has-beens on Instagram to see what useless products they are hawking after their thirty seconds of fame are over. Now with social media, you can extend your seconds and get paid to promote laxative teas. What a time to be alive!

As passionate as I am for reality TV, I have never wanted to be on it. Yet somehow, I ended up in the ultimate reality show, sharing four years of my relationship with millions of people. That's what I get for dating the King of YouTube.

Between the videos on both of our channels, our audiences got to experience our first Valentine's Day together, the first time we said I love you, the day we moved in together, and the moment we adopted our dog. Every intimate moment was documented and distributed. It wasn't that we were exploiting our relationship (although we both had a tendency to use clickbait titles like "MY GIRLFRIEND IS PREGNANT?!" with a picture of Shane holding my stomach and only later reveal we had just eaten too much and were having food babies); we were just intense workaholics who found it far easier and much more fun to work together. Not to mention the videos always did well because people loved us together (I never said the internet had good taste). At one point, I even had merchandise made with our couple name—"Shisa"—on it that sold incredibly well. I later learned *shisha* (which I realize is different but close enough that the internet mixes the two up) is a term for smoking tobacco out of a hookah. I feel a little guilty that there are still kids walking around wearing "Team Shisa" T-shirts. Say no to hookahs, guys. It seems cool for like a second when you turn eighteen, but I promise you, you'll end up looking like a totally tacky d-bag.

Rounding out our third year together, the relationship started wearing on both of us. At that point we had been living together for a year, but we were both so immersed in work that we unknowingly put our love life in the backseat. Shane also began to express feelings of depression and anxiety more than he had in the past. He would sleep all day and stay up all night. I began to think this was a direct result of me. Had I become unattractive or, worse, unlovable to him? If I was lucky I'd catch him between his slumber; we'd usually only talk about work or I'd complain about some chore he didn't do. I take the blame for getting annoyed with him and lashing out; that was certainly a by-product of my budding insecurities about my desirability.

On occasion, he would try to cheer me up by dancing for me, but it never worked. Him shaking his hips and sashaying around, doing his best *RuPaul's Drag Race* impressions, made me furious. Don't get me wrong, I love that show, but something about my boyfriend watching it religiously upset me. I'm pretty sure it's because I knew. Instead of having an open conversation about it, I just buried it and got angry when he would leave the fridge door open or forget to put the toilet seat down. All things that wouldn't typically bother me, but I was upset because he was upset, and neither of us wanted to dig deep and talk about why.

I was adamant about Shane going to therapy; I was worried about him. He didn't argue with me, mostly because he knew it was necessary. Plus, he had urged me to do the same early on in our relationship. We are both advocates of getting help when needed, yet even after he started counseling, his depression persisted. Together we eventually came to the conclusion that it would be healthier for us if he moved out. We were reluctant to call it a breakup because we didn't want to admit that it was over. We loved each other so much; we were best friends. So we held on, occasionally meeting up and hooking up, each time feeling emptier and sadder than the last.

Amplifying the pain was the fact that we were still posting videos and pictures as if we were a happy couple. It was miserable, but we decided to wait before we publicly announced our split. We wanted to give ourselves time to fully process and move on. In the past, there had been other YouTube couples who had gone through public breakups, and we had watched as they were brutally ostracized. Most of the time, the community would side with the more popular of the two, and the other person would just fade away. This was terrifying for me. Shane was far more liked than I was. I couldn't help but stress over the fact that my YouTube career could end in conjunction with my relationship. I hated that I had to think like that. Not only was I trying to wrap my head around this drawn-out breakup, but I was worried about my view count. It felt so shallow, but it was my reality, and it was heartbreaking. This went on for almost a year.

One afternoon, Shane was sitting on my new couch in our old apartment. I had sold all the furniture when he moved out, saged the place, and bought new things. That was my way of dealing with change without really having to change. Still, somehow everything felt old again whenever Shane was around. This time, though, we sat looking at each other with a new sense of understanding. (Maybe it was the sage.) This was the final goodbye talk. I knew it, he knew it, and we were both ready. Shane looked extra nervous. He was pale, beads of sweat had formed on his forehead, and he was visibly shaken.

"I need to tell you something," he said, his lip quivering, his eyes tearing.

My heart dropped into my stomach. It was in that moment that I knew. I mean, I always knew. But now, we both finally knew. It was confirmed.

I grabbed his hands, trying to provide reassurance for the both of us.

"I know," I said, nodding my head as I began to tear up. "I know."

We both started to cry. It was the moment we had been waiting for. Finally, I knew for certain that I hadn't done anything to push him away. Sure, I was a brat toward the end, but I wasn't unlovable or undesirable. He just needed to find his truth, the one he had been denying all these years. The truth that had caused him to crumble into a deep depression and withdraw from everything and everyone. Especially me. Finally, the air between us didn't feel heavy anymore. The expectations disappeared, and all that was left was our reality. I loved Shane. I loved him so much. I just wanted him to be happy. Even if it meant what I always knew it meant.

"I support you. I love you. You need to go experiment and do what you need to do to find your happiness," I said, or something along those lines. The moment is so ingrained in my head, but the details are blurred like a dream.

After we cried and hugged, and cried some more, we finally broached the subject of our public announcement. Again, I hate that this even had to come up after such a powerful, life-changing moment, but this was our reality. We decided we would meet on the upcoming Tuesday to film a video together and take that insane weight we had been carrying for so long off our shoulders. I was finally ready. I wanted to move on. I needed to move on. Even if it was terrifying and potentially a career killer.

Tuesday morning came. I texted Shane to see when he wanted to film and get this thing over with. He promptly wrote back.

I already made the video. I wanted to tell my coming-out story. I felt like I needed to. It's going up in two hours.

Two hours? As in, you only gave me two hours' notice that eight million people are going to find out that not only is my relationship over, but also my boyfriend is bisexual? A whole year of stressing about how this day would go, spiraling into different possible outcomes, each one bringing me into a stronger state of panic? A whole year of sadness and confusion and fear reduced to a two-hour warning that was completely out of my control? A whole year of hiding and pretending, hoping no one would catch on? Two hours, and my life would officially be scrambled and there was nothing I could do about it?

I wrote back, biting my tongue.

Um, ok. I thought we were doing this together.

Shane typed back.

This is my story to tell.

He wasn't wrong. He also wasn't completely right.

Enter full-blown panic attack. I quickly texted my best friends—I needed help. I couldn't do this alone. Even I, who prefers to deal with things by myself, knew that.

Guys. Shane is putting a video up in two hours, outing himself and our relationship.

The phone rang quickly thereafter.

"Leave the phone at home. I'm taking you out," Randi demanded. She had spoken with Jessica. My two best friends were teaching a summer course together and decided that Jessica would stay and work for the both of them, and Randi would take me out. They both knew how emotionally taxing this was going to be and wanted to be sure I stayed as far away from social media as possible.

Randi picked me up, and without many words we drove up the Pacific Coast Highway. The windows were down, the wind was blowing through my hair, and the tears were rolling down my face at a steady pace. We ended up at some bar, staring at the ocean. All I wanted was to not remember, to numb my brain and my heart. Oh, and French fries. I only wanted French fries. So it began. My day of forgetting, one vodka and fry at a time.

At one point, Randi took me down the road to a place called the Self Realization Center. It's a gorgeous piece of land with a garden and a pond. A place where people go to reflect, meditate, find peace, and get grounded (very LA). Probably not a place suitable for a wasted, heartbroken mess, but at the time, it seemed appropriate. I just remember staring at the turtles, whose bodies were submerged in the water, but their heads were popping up just above the surface. All I could think was, "I'm one of those turtles. Even though most of me is drowning, I can still keep my head above water. I got this."

Who knew vodka and French fries would result in such insight? Randi and I bought each other turtle key chains in the gift shop before we left. It was a way to remember my self-realization and to serve as proof the next morning that we had actually been there, that it wasn't all just some fucked-up dream.

We headed back that night to our local bar to meet up with Jessica, because god knows I needed another drink. At one point, I sloppily announced to the waitress, "A round of shots for the table! My boyfriend just came out of the closet!"

I'm pretty certain that round was on the house. Maybe even our whole tab was covered that night. Everyone just felt so bad for me. I was clearly a mess, but my friends encouraged me to have this day. To cry, stuff my face, and drown my sorrow. To be angry and sad, mad and confused. To do what I needed to do, knowing I was safe because they were taking care of me. Knowing that sometimes you have to hit your rock bottom to give yourself the space to climb to the top all over again. I'll never truly be able to express how much my friends meant to me that day. Thank you, guys. I love you. My liver, however, doesn't.

When I got home, I stumbled into bed, finally ready to watch Shane's video. I picked up my phone, clicked on the video link, took a deep breath, and pressed Play. My heart sank, anticipating that everything was about to change for me. With one click of that Play button, I would turn what had felt like a bad dream into an actual reality.

I watched intently through my tear-filled eyes as he spoke about his struggles with depression, how it wore on our relationship, and his realization that he had been burying something inside him for years. My heart raced the moment he finally revealed the secret he had been keeping from everyone, even himself. Surprisingly, with his reveal came a sense of relief, not only from him on the screen, but from me in that moment. The lies were over, and the truth was out there. A huge weight was lifted; I continued to watch the video with a little less fear. He spoke with such honesty and bravery, mastering the art of telling the truth and spreading a message. He spoke warmly of me and our relationship and my part in this life-changing moment. It was more beautiful than I could have ever imagined.

I hung on to every word. As much as I wanted to be mad at him, all I felt was complete pride. I knew within seconds of watching that his bravery and honesty were going to change lives and help so many kids in similar situations. I had never loved him more than I did in that moment. I don't remember much after that, other than checking to see what people were saying about me in the comments. I was relieved when I noticed that the majority of people were thanking me for supporting him and helping him come to his truth. I won't ever take credit for that, but I was grateful for the overwhelming generosity. Of course, there were comments that said, "There go her views," and things of that sort, which I had expected, considering the internet is full of troll demons. Overall, though, the consensus was positive. I could finally stop holding my breath. I fell asleep with the phone in my hand and slept for what felt like forever.

As days and weeks passed, the wounds healed, and my fears lessened. Shane eventually apologized for the unfair two-hour warning. I understood. No one can properly prepare for something like this. We were just navigating the way we knew how, with everyone watching. What a life.

Even now, I still have no regrets. I came out of those four years a far better person for it. Sure, I have some scars that won't seem to fade. I'm always fearful that any man I'm with will eventually want to experiment with his sexuality too. Overall, the good outweighs the bad. I learned so much from my time with Shane. He was and continues to be my YouTube mentor, pushing me to constantly reinvent myself in order to keep my content fresh. Thanks to him, I've learned how to keep a joke going, leave better tips, go days without showering, angle my camera to look skinnier, and eat Chipotle in record time.

Most of all, I've gained empathy and clarity for the way relationships work and, more specifically, how breakups work. Which brings me back to the cliché I began this chapter with. If there is one takeaway about breakups that I'd like to share with you, it's that they can be handled with grace and maturity if you keep your ego out of it. Everyone deserves a chance at true happiness and unwavering love, no matter their age. If you can help facilitate that for someone else by letting them go, then you are not only allowing that person the space to find their truth, you are allowing yourself that opportunity as well. Sure, it hurts. Sure, you wanted it to work. Sure, you don't want to be alone, especially if you're in your thirties. But it is selfish to try to deny the reality and force a false truth. Besides, online dating is pretty easy to figure out. Literally every moron is doing it!

Everyone kept calling me a "hero" after Shane came out. I was honored by this but would never take that title.

That's reserved for the best of the best. What I did end up saying in a video on my channel, which made much more sense to me, was…

"I'm just a girl who loved a boy who didn't love himself. So I let him go." That's something I'm proud to say I was able to do. Because in the end, it gave us both a better chance at true happiness.

Shane and I are still the best of friends. He is currently in a long-term relationship with a lovely man, whom I adore. I've never seen him happier. In fact, I've never seen him more himself. It's a weird thing to be so elated for an ex's new relationship, but there's relief in knowing that we made the right decision. This is the life he was meant to live. Every so often, we meet up for lunch and chat about work, our families, and my dating life. I tell him stories of the crazies I've gone out with. He cackles and tries to give me relationship advice. I take it with a grain of salt. After all, I taught him everything he knows. We laugh, then we laugh some more, and then we part ways. I go home to continue swiping left and right on another dating app. I do it now without fear or hesitation, because I know I was able to survive the Titanic of all internet-dating experiences. I will keep trying, despite all the insane dating stories, because I still have hope that I will find someone who will change my life the way Shane did. Minus the liking-boys part, and hopefully the millions-of-people-watching part too. But who knows? For now, my life continues to feel like a pretty addictive reality show. Bring on the poop tea sponsorships!

Wine and Nuts: My Night with a Hollywood Legend

Hi. I'm miserable.

—Elaine Benes

I truly believe people come into your life for a reason. I know it sounds cheesy, like a slogan you'd find on every piece of merchandise in a Hallmark store, but it's hard to deny once you start paying attention to the lessons you've gained from the people throughout your life. These experiences can come from someone you've known and admired your whole life, or a stranger you exchange kind words with as you grab your latte on the way to work. The takeaways may be as mind-blowing as learning that I am susceptible to losing myself in order to make others happy, or relatively minor, like, Bed Bath & Beyond 10 percent off coupons never expire. Thank you, lady in the bath mat aisle several years ago, for giving me that literally price-less nugget of wisdom.

I'm not saying every interaction is significant, but it's interesting to reflect back and extract whatever useful tidbits you can apply to your life moving forward. Even when a relationship goes south, you can at least say you got something out of it. You know what I mean?

I was pulling out of a driveway the other day, when I saw a kind-looking man in a turban do a double take as he crossed in front of my car. He put his hands together in a prayer pose and brought them to his third eye (the space between your two eyes where your "higher consciousness" lives, according to some). Then, as if we had a telepathic understanding, he walked up to my window just as I was rolling it down for him. Side note: Don't roll windows down for strangers—it's a potentially very dangerous thing to do. I blame my lapse of judgment on the Californian part of me that believes the opportunity for a mystical encounter lurks around every corner. Nevertheless, I felt like this man and I were destined to meet, and by the look in his eyes, he must have had some message from "the other side" he needed to share with me.

Once my window was all the way down, the man, without so much as a breath or hello, began to speak. His voice was low and gentle, his cadence slow and methodical. I listened closely, 90 percent sure he was harmless but clenching my butt cheeks on behalf of the other 10 percent that was fearful he wanted to kill me or, worse, tell me my career was going nowhere.

I've never been overly curious about my future in terms of marriage or babies; such an exercise is futile in my book. What I am constantly pondering and stressing about, though, is the trajectory of my career. I was hopeful in this moment that this was finally going to be my divine career-guiding intervention.

"You have a very kind soul," he said. "You are always willing to help others. But when you need help, no one is there."

"Ouch. But, like, yeah. Kind of," I said, wondering if we could fast-forward to the employment portion of this routine.

"You have digestion problems," he said, moving his flattened palm in a circular motion around his belly. He would have been a bit more accurate had he pointed to his asshole.

"Spot-on," I said, as I held in a fart.

"You are very lucky," he said with certainty. I HAVE been receiving free *Travel + Leisure* magazines these past few months for some reason. Nothing makes you feel more leisurely than reading about travel from the comfort of your toilet.

"Your love life is unreadable." Now I really believed him.

"Your career…well, I have so much more to say. Why don't you come with me, and I will tell you more," he said, pointing in the direction of an unmarked building.

I may think I have a sixth sense, but even someone with only one sense would know that following a stranger into a seemingly vacant structure is a terrible idea.

"Oh, no. I can't today. But thank you," I said, quickly realizing this wasn't the kismet consultation I was banking on.

"You'll get a free gemstone," he said, lifting his eyebrow as if he just used the greatest pickup line of all time. I'm not going to lie—I was tempted. I love a gemstone and I LOVE free shit.

"Sorry. I gotta go, but what was that thing about my career you were going to say?" I asked while giving him my best "I'm pretending like I don't know your marketing scheme in order to get you to spill the beans about the future of my work life" face.

"Maybe next time," he said, pointing back to the mysterious, empty building.

That 10 percent butt-clenching instinct was right; he wasn't trying to kill me, but he surely was killing my chance at getting a proper (and free) answer regarding the path of my career. Part of me wonders if he actually knew where I was headed but withheld the information because it wasn't looking great for me. I guess I'll have to wait to find out, or dish out the cash for another reading and a potential death wish.

I did get close to peering into my future another time, though. Shockingly, it didn't involve palm readers, astrologers, or strangers in turbans. All it took was me, several bottles of wine, a handful of nuts, and a Hollywood legend. Who could have predicted that?

I was on set for the first "big" job I booked, when I met her, the Hollywood legend I will from now on refer to as Ms. Legend. Up until this point I had been working on smaller-scale projects, so my nerves were on fire knowing I'd be acting alongside one of the best in the business (not to say my grandma, who gamely tackles anything I force her into on my YouTube channel, isn't the best). This was THE comedy icon I had always looked up to, daydreamed about having the same career, and prayed would take me under her wing to teach me the "ways of Hollywood." I never actually thought it would happen; when it did, I literally had to pinch myself. Humble brag, I know, but the truth was I had become crippled with anxiety weeks before meeting her, thinking I wouldn't be able to handle the pressure.

Much to my surprise, when we met on set for the first time, I instantly felt at ease. Maybe it was her effervescent personality or the fact that she told me she was familiar with my work (to this day I'm not sure if she actually was, but I appreciated the graceful lie); either way, she made me feel confident that I'd have her support as I made this giant career step.

We spent the next four months working side by side. I studied her every move. The way she said her lines, commanded the set, exhaled her Virginia Slims. I wanted to soak in as much as I could, not miss a single detail, because I knew watching her would be better than any master class I'd ever overpay for.

Being on set for that long bonded us like family. She was instinctively protective of me, and I was undeniably in awe of her. There was also an unspoken understanding that we needed each other. Never in a million years did I think someone like her would need someone like me, but with the rise of social media came the fall of her relevance.

She hadn't been working as much as she used to and knew full well an increase in her social presence could help get her back "in the game." Insert eye roll here if you must, but she wasn't wrong. Somehow over the course of the last few years, the number of followers you have across your social pages has become just as important, if not more, as your years of experience actively working in Hollywood. It's so backward, and so unfair, but this is the reality. It's also how I got here.

After we finished our project, she extended an invitation for me to join her at her remote home in the Malibu Hills to celebrate and "discuss a potential future together." Not like a marriage; she swears she will never get "fucking married" again. She was suggesting we build a creative partnership to put our brains and expertise together, to come up with a new project that would launch (or in her case, relaunch) our careers. I realize that I sound so blasé saying that, but believe me, I was shitting my pants. Oh crap, what was I going to wear?

After a solid twenty minutes driving in circles, trying to find the private location, my Uber pulled up to a giant mansion in the Hills. I stepped out in my kitten heels and sensible blazer, holding an expensive bottle of wine I had carefully researched, hoping I wouldn't look like a total millennial who drinks wine out of a can. Seriously, it's the new boxed wine. Move over, Franzia! You've been millennialized.

I looked at the luxurious home in front of me, pinching myself that this was actually happening. "Don't fuck this up," I whispered under my breath. I had a list of pitches in the "notes" app on my phone that I had planned on casually presenting her with at some point that evening. I didn't want to appear desperate, but I also didn't want to forget anything. I figured a casual note in the phone made me look creative but hip. Oh Jesus, I was gonna fuck this up.

As I approached the front door, I could hear barking coming from the left wing of the house. Yes, I said wing. Fancy people's houses have those. Wings are typically add-ons to the main structure and make the owner feel better about themselves. Kind of like how guys with small penises drive big trucks. I imagine most of the time these wings aren't even used. They just sit there alone, filled with plastic-covered furniture, waiting for the house-keeper to come and clean them, even though there isn't anything to clean. The only semblance of a wing I have in my place is that one corner behind the fridge that I can never reach; it just sits there alone, covered in dust.

The front door had a note taped onto it that read, "Lisa, come through the side door," in messy handwriting. I looked to my left and then to my right, realizing there were literally four or five doors this note could apply to. I heard a faint shouting accompanied by the nonstop bark-ing a few doors down to my left: "Over here! Over here!" It was hard to make out which exact door the sounds were coming from. You know when you hear the smoke detec-tor incessantly beep for a new battery (which, by the way, only seems to happen in the middle of the night) but can't figure out which damn detector it's coming from? You can stand under one and be convinced it's the culprit, just to then hear the beep jump to another room. Her shouting felt like that until I noticed that one of the doors was slightly ajar. I saw Ms. Legend herself peering through the crack, holding back the dog who amazingly was responsible for all the commotion.

"Never mind," she said, struggling to keep the dog from charging at me. "Go back to the front door." I wasn't even in the house yet, and I was already having a confusing yet strangely good time. I felt like I was on some weird scavenger hunt, excited to see what my next clue was going to be.

Back where I started, the giant front door burst open. I was expecting to see the lady I had worked with for the past few months but was taken aback when I was greeted by someone else. It was still Ms. Legend, but a stripped-down version. No makeup, hair up, an unexceptional outfit, and bare feet. She was in her natural habitat, and I was way overdressed.

"Come in! Come in!" she said, waving me through and practically pushing me into the next dark room. I felt like I was suddenly in *Alice in Wonderland*, and she was the Cheshire Cat, leading me down the rabbit hole.

"I brought you this. Thank you for having me," I said, eagerly presenting her the bottle of wine I had splurged on.

Without stopping to take a breath, she began talking quickly. She was stringing together sentences as if punctuation were a simple, petty suggestion. I'm not sure if she was nervous (which would be ironic, considering how many times I peed before I got there), or if this was just how she spoke when she wasn't in work mode. Either way, I tried my best to follow along and keep up.

"Oh thanks what do you want to drink this is my favorite good if we have this?" she asked as she pulled out a Meiomi Pinot Noir. I recognized that bottle right away. It's an eighteen-dollar bottle. A delicious eighteen-dollar bottle, but an eighteen-dollar bottle. You mean to tell me that I could have only spent eighteen dollars, and I would have won her over? Is it too late to take back the sixty-dollar one I brought? Is this what it feels like when you buy someone an expensive piece of jewelry you have carefully picked out, but they end up always wearing the jewelry you randomly got them from some dude on the street when you were drunk in Mexico?

I nodded yes, because she began talking again before I got a chance to actually verbalize my answer. At this point I was going with my theory that she was experiencing some social butterflies. I've come to learn that most actors are actually pretty shy in their real lives. Now that we didn't have a crew surrounding us, or a script to talk about, the pressure to socialize was on. As she opened the bottle with her electric bottle opener, she proclaimed, "I just started a new medication for weight loss and overall happiness, so I'm not sure how it's going to interact with drinking!" Welp. There's the real answer.

Pop! The cork was out, and I was now in a complete panic thinking I would have to resuscitate this woman at some point during our evening together. I should have paid more attention in that Red Cross babysitting training class I took when I was twelve.

Clearly, she wasn't worried, because she filled our glasses to the very top. Truthfully, I was pretty relieved to have a large glass of antinerve juice myself. What a combo we were. She offered me pistachios and apologized for not having any other food. She explained she was on a strict delivery diet and had nothing else in her house. She led me to her kitchen, to give me a tour of her barren fridge. I'm not sure if she wanted to prove to me that she wasn't lying about her lack of food, or if she was proud to show off her diet-friendly fridge, but I felt like I was in an episode of *Cribs* and I was stoked about it.

"Shit, I forgot I just got a new water filter, and I need to turn the faucet on for five minutes to set it up," she said out of nowhere. She quickly did so, then took my arm and guided me into yet another room. I could hear the water rushing in the sink.

At this point, as she led me around her perfectly designed home, I began to wonder when we were going to sit down and talk business. Don't get me wrong; I was enjoying this brain-jumbling journey so far. Her energy, though incredibly frenetic, was beyond charming and entertaining. But as much fun as I was having trying to keep up with her, I was really looking forward to picking her brilliant brain.

After romping through the majority of the downstairs rooms, jumping from one conversation to another, we landed in a gorgeous living room that looked like it had been plucked straight from the Restoration Hardware catalog. Short of having plastic on all the couches to preserve them, the room was as perfect as a museum exhibit. Nothing appeared to have been touched or sat on ever, but here we were now, sitting at the gorgeous table draped in a perfectly pressed gold-trimmed tablecloth. Ms. Legend poured us both another glass of wine and pushed a fresh bowl of pistachios toward me.

Finally, we broached the subject of acting. She did most of the talking as I unshelled my dinner. I didn't mind her yapping; in fact, I preferred it. The pressure for me to pitch my half-developed ideas dissolved when I realized she didn't actually want to talk about "our future"—she just wanted to share tales of the "Wild West" (her nickname for Hollywood). She started in on one story about a fellow actor and a project they did that went terribly wrong. With every detail of the story, she grew more and more enraged, as if she were experiencing it for the first time. I listened, hanging on to every word, popping pistachios in my mouth like popcorn. When it came to the part of the story when she decided to stand her ground, walk into the producer's office, and give him hell, she stood up before me and, with complete seriousness, acted out the entire conversation. She literally switched roles, from producer to her younger self, back and forth, back and forth, with a dialogue that went on for a solid twenty minutes. It was slightly manic but also the performance of a lifetime. I was mesmerized. What struck me the most, besides her phenomenal character work, was her ability to recall every detail of that specific conversation. In fact, she could remember all the details from that production even though it happened so many years ago. Pretty incredible, considering I can't even remember what I did yesterday. After she settled back in and took a breath, she pulled out a pack of cigarettes.

"Do you mind? I don't normally smoke in the house, but since my kid is at his dad's, FUCK IT." She lit the cigarette before I even had time to answer. I'm guessing it was a rhetorical question. This bitch does what she wants.

I've always been fascinated by rich people who smoke in their gorgeous homes. It's one thing to smoke in your dingy apartment, because who cares? You've already succumbed to the fact that you are living in a shithole with thin walls and carpet that needed to be replaced fifteen years ago. What's a little cigarette smoke going to do at this point? The smell of cat piss from the person who lived there prior will surely overpower the smoke scent. On the other hand, why would you pay millions of dollars for your very own catalog-worthy home if you were going to muck it up with the smell of a Vegas casino?

I once dated a guy whose family was very wealthy. East Coast yuppies. He brought me home for Christmas one year, and I was awestruck when I entered their perfectly staged home. I remember the crisp white lines and the symmetrical bookshelves, the carefully placed entryway benches, and the decadent dining room table with a floral centerpiece that must have cost more than my round-trip ticket.

Three-quarters of the way through the Christmas Eve dinner, after the third course but before dessert, his mother pulled out a pack of cigarettes. Without so much as a flinch from anyone else, she began to smoke. Ashing her long, thin nicotine stick into a crystal ashtray. No cracking of the window, or lighting of a candle. Just utter disregard for anything other than filling her lungs with her favorite toxins. Without a word, her husband pushed back his chair and stood up. I assumed he was going to open a window or door to provide some ventilation, but instead he grabbed his coveted box of cigars and lit up too. One for him, and one for his son. The whole room filled with smoke, and I suddenly felt like I was in a Coppola film. I don't remember much more after that due to the white port that was served (which is the most rich-white-person thing they could ever serve), but the next morning the house looked perfect, as if it had never been touched, and it smelled of wild gardenias, as if the night before had never happened. How the beautifully papered walls resisted the thick scent of cigarette and cigar smoke, I'll never know. Maybe it was a Christmas miracle. Or more likely, the in-house staff, who looked as if they had been up all night, had scrubbed our filth away.

Back to Ms. Legend's now smoke-filled living room. As the night went on and we drank more wine and devoured more nuts, I began to understand the person behind the legend. I know—it sounds like another "woo-woo" moment, but it was the truth. I think many times celebrities aren't given much of an identity beyond that title of celebrity. We forget that they are humans whose public persona is typically only a fraction of their true self, a mask to protect them from the outside world. Many times we are completely unaware of their inner struggles because we equate fame and fortune with happiness. In that moment, though, I forgot that Ms. Legend was a legend. Instead she was just a raw and honest woman, sitting before me, sharing her emotional journey, most of which I could totally relate to. Sure, I didn't have a career like hers, or a tornado of a personality, and I could never match her claims of "giving fantastic head." (I kid you not, she told me this and began to explain her technique, but I promptly changed the subject.) What spoke to me were her ongoing fears of leaving the house, her overwhelming desire to "be alone forever" because her trust in men was tarnished after years of being "fucked over," and her everlasting feelings of being "different" than most of her peers. I felt like I was looking into a mirror of my future self, realizing that our emotional hurdles were almost as similar as our fabulous cheekbones. I'm pretty sure she was feeling the connection too because she grabbed my hand, looked deeply into my eyes, and told me I reminded her of herself at my age and that she loved me. Promptly afterward, she peed with the bathroom door wide open. That was the moment I realized this utterly eccentric and unapologetic woman was my spirit animal.

Near the end of our fifth hour drinking and soul-searching, Ms. Legend handed me her home phone and told me to call for a ride. It was a pretty abrupt ending to the night, but at the same time it was perfect. We had both reached the end of our socializing threshold, and there was no point in pretending otherwise. I told her I'd wait outside for the Uber just in case they had trouble finding the house. She opened the front door, hugged me goodbye, and without so much as a breath, shut it behind me. As I walked to the street, I noticed all of her house lights went off at once. She was done for the night. Maybe even for the week. I think I was too.

As I sat in the car on the way home, I attempted to reflect on what the hell had just happened. I also realized she never turned off the kitchen sink. I wanted to laugh but also cry. I related to this woman on so many levels but also hurt so deeply for her. Here she was, a mega movie star in a giant home, with all the great successes and incredible opportunities I'd kill for, and yet at the end of the day she was left swirling in her complicated brain, isolated in her fort, self-medicating to ease the pain, with all the lights off. Is this what I had been striving for all these years? Is this why I push myself to audition even though it sends me into an emotional tailspin? Is this the reason I incessantly diet and exercise, beating myself up if I mess either one up? If I were to achieve the career I've been desperately chasing, is this what my future would look like? More urgently, what's that water bill going to look like?

I never saw her again after that night. We are still in touch, but I'm guessing after she sobered up and realized I got a proper peek into the "real" her, she may have been scared off. Or maybe I was just terrible company—who knows? All I do know is after that experience I stopped paying for psychics. I caught a glimpse of my future that night, and that was way more than enough. Not that it deterred me from continuing to fight for my dream career, but it did remind me that if I didn't actively work on my issues now, no amount of success in the future would make them better. In fact, I could end up in a pretty dark place. I called my therapist the next day.

Certain people come into your life for a reason. Ms. Legend came into mine like a whirlwind, and now I smile knowing why. She gave me a handful of lessons that I still carry with me and remind myself of, especially whenever I feel down or stressed about my future. Maybe some of them will resonate with you and your journey:

One: Success does not lead to happiness. You can be the most famous person in the world and still hurt. One must do the internal work to thrive, regardless of how great things might look on the outside.

Two: You don't have to be like everyone else. In fact, success flourishes with individuality. Stop wasting your time trying to conform to the way you think you're supposed to be, and start accepting the fact that you are a precious and valuable weirdo. Never apologize for that.

Three: Relationships are hard. Sadly, there are people out there who just want to take advantage of you. Listen to your gut. Protect your heart. Hold your family and friends close. If you aren't sure if someone loves you for you, pee with the door open. You'll learn quickly where they stand.

Four: No one can predict your future, because you make your own future. Sure, there are paths I believe you are destined to go down, but it's up to you to decide how you will emotionally travel through them. You can dive in with grace and dignity, or you can cannon-bomb with anger and self-righteousness. Your choices will dictate where you ultimately land.

And lastly: I now know for certain that eighteen-dollar wine is just as well received as sixty-dollar wine. Save your cash.

The Wedding Circuit

I hate being at a table alone with a married couple talking about their married friends and their married furniture.

—Elaine Benes

I went to seven weddings in one year—this is not an exaggeration for dramatic effect. This is the reality. By the time you hit thirty, everyone is already married or sending you a save-the-date to their upcoming wedding. If you didn't already feel insecure about being without a partner or a ring on that finger, wait till you get to the third wedding when the mother of the bride drunkenly corners you in the bathroom and tells you she feels bad for you because you aren't engaged yet. Really, weddings aren't for the fainthearted.

Wedding One was the best of the year. Not because I was enthralled with the couple's undying love for each other, or because the appetizers were ample and delicious, but simply because it was the first in the wedding circuit and I was still very naïve. At that point, I thought these celebrations were a fun excuse to get dressed up, drink for free, and dance off the enormous number of calories I consumed inhaling those delicious pigs in a blanket. Who created those? They are truly the world's greatest gift in a tiny, crispy package.

I was a bridesmaid in Wedding Two. There's no greater honor than being asked to stand next to your childhood friends as they say their vows. No greater expense either. Not only are you breaking the bank buying a kitchen gadget that you know the couple is never going to use (still unclear why they registered for a two-hundred-dollar bread maker, considering one of them gets hives just looking at gluten), but you also have to invest in a dress that you will NEVER wear again. No matter how you try to style it, that burnt sienna taffeta sack that you had to buy from J.Crew for a hundred and fifty bucks will never work. In fact, you're better off not even trying to make it work—it didn't look good on you to begin with. At least the maid of honor stopped throwing a hissy fit because she thought the other dresses we tried on "made her look fat." That bitch honestly looked incredible in everything, but no matter how great we told her she looked, she refused to believe us. If an aggressively hued zipped-up trash bag finally made her happy and got her to shut up, it was worth every penny.

Wedding Three is a bit of a blur. Probably because I spent most of it arguing with Shane. I wanted him to dance with me, but he just wanted to sit and eat cake. This exact conversation happened at every wedding we went to from there on out. I think the pressure of not being married like everyone else was starting to get to me, so I chose to argue with him about the Macarena instead of dealing with the real issue. I knew I wasn't keen on getting engaged, but it was hard to avoid the pressure of everyone constantly asking me when I was going to be, shoving the institution of marriage in my face over and over again. All Shane was shoving in his face was cake. In retrospect, he was on to something. That was a far more satisfying way of dealing with it all.

Even if I wasn't in the midst of a wedding circuit, I'd feel the unavoidable stress to take this next step. Marriage is ingrained in all of us from a very young age. According to the stories we grew up on, people meet, fall in love, get married, and live happily ever after. I just assumed this was what everyone was expected to do. Like brushing our teeth, graduating from high school, and not driving off a cliff.

As if treating marriage like a typical rite of passage doesn't evoke enough pressure, girls and women alike are constantly being sold on the fantasy of the "beautiful bride." From princess movies to shows like *Say Yes to the Dress*, it's hard to avoid the message that being a bride is the most crucial moment in your life. Hell, when I was six, I dressed up as a bride for Halloween. What kind of twisted, brainwashed shit is that? Why on earth would a six-year-old choose that? It ended up raining heavily that year; I believe this was Mother Nature's ironic nod to my future.

I just read that the global wedding industry is worth something close to three hundred billion dollars. This is not a fucking joke. All that money is being poured into a single day that we are told we are supposed to have. So, the next time someone tells you to ignore the pressures to get married, flick them off three hundred billion times. It's impossible. It's like telling a dog not to lick its own dick. It's right there; you can't avoid it. Although, unlike marriage, licking your own dick sounds great.

My initial aversion to marriage was planted years before I went on this seven-wedding-party journey. I'm certain it stemmed from having divorced parents. Right? That seems like an obvious explanation I don't need to overpay my therapist to tell me. My parents split when I was eighteen, but they fought throughout my childhood. I would lay with my ear pressed up to the bottom of my bedroom door, right where the hallway light shone through, and listen to them scream at each other. I don't have a memory of what they were saying, just that it always ended with the sound of the garage door opening, my dad's car turning on, and then the garage door closing. Sometimes I would shut my eyes real tight and wish he wouldn't come back. Not because I didn't love him, but because I didn't want them to fight anymore.

Why would I want to put myself in a position where I could feel the same kind of pain my parents experienced? Just so I can fulfill some fantasy I read about when I was a kid, or check off a box on the "standard life" timeline? Sure, my parents' separation was the mature and appropriate measure that led to a wonderful co-parenting friendship and a happier life for both of them. In fact, their approach to divorce is what the young kids on the internet would refer to as "goals." Still, I could never wholeheartedly accept the idea that we are all supposed to get married, even if attending weddings often hypnotized me to feel otherwise.

Ironically, the couple from Wedding Three ended up getting a divorce not long after the party. Nothing more upsetting than seeing your friends split. Nothing, except having just spent money on a gift for that couple. Shouldn't we get it back? Or at least decide which member of the couple gets to keep it? I should have the right to decide where the attachable bidet I got them (seriously, they registered for this) should go. If you're going to get divorced, it's only fair I get to pick whose ass gets a daily shot of water.

Wedding Four was a hot mess. The florist never showed, so the bride's family ransacked the surrounding areas for whatever shrubbery they could bundle together and call a bouquet. Due to the hour-long scavenger hunt, by the time we all sat down for the outdoor ceremony, more than half the attendees were sunburnt and dehydrated. Needless to say, the minute the booze entered everyone's frail and thirsty bodies, the number of obnoxious drunk cousins that decided they wanted to make an "off the cuff" speech was unbelievable. I knew Italians had big families, but I didn't realize one person could have THAT many cousins. After what felt like four hours of sloppy speeches that involved lots of "shout-outs" to some other unbuttoned, gold-chain-clad drunk at table number six, we decided to leave. I have a feeling the speeches are still going.

By Wedding Five, it was clear that every wedding was pretty much the same. Yes, there were little nuances, like a taco truck, that made each one "different," but ultimately, they were all just a series of scheduled moments chained together to create the "perfect" night. They ran like clockwork.

4:30 p.m.
Arrive at event and regret you wore heels as you sink into the grass.

Chat with your friend's friends who you would otherwise avoid.

Sit in uncomfortable chairs and wonder why they haven't served the booze yet.

4:45 p.m.
Check your watch and realize they are starting late and you totally had time to pee.

Obsess over the fact that you really have to pee, but now it's probably too late to pee.

5:08 p.m.
Some classical music begins and everyone shuts up except that one crying baby.

The family members walk down the aisle all done up. It makes you uncomfortable because now you are attracted to your friend's parents.

The groom walks in, freshly shaven and looking like an actual man. Not the hungover beast in shorts and flip-flops you know him as.

A gaggle of girls in matching dresses and weird side braids waddle down in their high heels and plastered smiles.

5:10 p.m.
A different classical song comes on, a little louder, and you all stand up. Except for the old uncle in the front with the walker.

The bride enters, looking pretty and perfect and clearly overwhelmed.

Up come the phones to capture the moment. No one considers being in the actual moment.

5:11 p.m.
The ceremony begins and you hang on every word, because you're a sap and you want to believe in all this.

You look over to see your boyfriend checking his Instagram. You suddenly don't believe in all this.

5:19 p.m.

The couple says their vows, and you regret not buying waterproof mascara. You believe in all this again.

5:25 p.m.

The couple kisses; everyone cheers. Mostly for the couple, but also because it's time to drink and eat tiny food.

5:30 p.m.

Your boyfriend stands close to the kitchen door so he can get first dibs on the grub.

You stand in the longest bar line ever, forced to small-talk with the weird aunt waiting behind you.

5:34 p.m.

You have to explain to Weird Aunt that you are not married, or engaged, or even very close.

5:36 p.m.

You order two vodka sodas with a lime. Both are for you. Your boyfriend doesn't drink, and you aren't waiting in that line again.

5:45 p.m.

You are pissed that you keep missing the mini grilled-cheese sandwiches because you got stuck in a conversation with your friend's old neighbor who you've never met but who knows everything about you due to her extensive Facebook stalking.

5:56 p.m.
You look for your table assignment and pray you aren't stuck next to people you don't like.

5:57 p.m.
You are stuck next to people you don't like.

6:15 p.m.
The DJ announces the bride and groom.

They make a grand entrance that they worked so hard on in hopes of it going viral.

You pray the waiters will come by with wine.

6:18 p.m.
The parents of the bride make a speech.

6:24 p.m.
The groom's brother makes a speech.

6:30 p.m.
The bride's sister makes a speech.

6:34 p.m.
The drunk frat bro tries to make a coherent speech.

6:37 p.m.
Two bridesmaids make a joint speech that includes them taking a popular song and changing the lyrics to personalize it for the newlyweds. You are transported to summer camp, and you hated summer camp.

6:43 p.m.
The father-daughter dance begins.

You sneak back to the bar.

6:50 p.m.
Dinner comes. Chicken, steak, or some bird food for the vegetarians.

You make small talk with the people your friends thought you had something in common with, but you totally don't have anything in common with.

Your boyfriend doesn't engage; he's too busy checking his phone.

7:15 p.m.
The DJ plays "Celebration."

You tap your foot and then are embarrassed that you like that song.

7:18 p.m.
You take a shot with Weird Aunt and realize she's the cool aunt.

7:25 p.m.
The DJ plays "Love Shack," and suddenly you are on the dance floor thinking you're Beyoncé's backup dancer. You're feeling your damn self again.

7:45 p.m.
You're fully drenched in sweat and decide hydrating means having another alcoholic beverage.

You head back to the bar and see all the regulars there.

You schmooze nonsense with the other boozers and think you are so fun.

8:15 p.m.
You stumble back to your table where your boyfriend is still sitting and on his phone.

You try to get him to dance, but he hates dancing.

You get mad and tell him he is no fun.

He tells you, "You're drunk."

You say, "No I'm not." Then you trip over yourself as you march back to the dance floor.

8:30 p.m.
You are bumping and grinding with the bride to Usher's "Yeah!"

You think you are a good dancer.

8:34 p.m.
You hug the bride for too long and tell her how much you love her and how fucking proud you are of her for taking this big step and how you wish you were her. It gets weird.

8:45 p.m.
You find the photo booth, pile in with a bunch of strangers, and throw up a peace sign. You don't know why you did that.

8:47 p.m.
You do another photo booth session, by yourself.

You think you're clever.

8:50 p.m.
You do another photo booth session, by yourself.

You flash the camera.

8:51 p.m.
You get escorted out of the photo booth.

9:03 p.m.
You go back to the bar to get a drink because you're mad, but you forget why.

You think you're best friends with the bartender.

9:05 p.m.
The bride and groom cut the cake. Only half the party pays attention.

9:13 p.m.
You make your way back to the table.

Your boyfriend is eating cake and looking at his phone.

9:20 p.m.
The DJ plays "Sweet Caroline." Everyone sings along.

9:45 p.m.
People start leaving.

Your boyfriend asks if you can go.

You tell him he's a party pooper.

The room starts to spin.

9:50 p.m.

The DJ plays Daft Punk's "One More Time," and you close down the dance floor with the last few survivors.

10:00 p.m.

Your boyfriend carries you back to the car as you start asking if you guys are ever going to get married.

10:03 p.m.

Regardless of his answer, you decide to pick a fight.

10:45 p.m.

You stumble into the house and eat whatever you can find.

10:50 p.m.

You tell your boyfriend you're sorry and you love him but also, he should dance at weddings.

10:51 p.m.

You take off all your clothes in the middle of the living room.

10:59 p.m.

You pass out on the couch.

11:35 p.m.

You wake up and forget where you are.

You stumble back to your room.

11:39 p.m.

You pass out in your bed, hoping you locked the front door.

That's how they all went, over and over again. After Wedding Five, Shane and I broke up. The breakup wasn't a direct result of the wedding circuit (see "My Gay Boyfriend"), but seeing the pending and endless save-the-dates on the fridge certainly pushed the process along. It's like when you know Christmas is coming, so you break up before you have to buy your soon-to-be ex a nice gift. You say cheap, I say proactive.

Wedding Six came so quickly after my breakup that I had already RSVP'd for the two of us. Not only did I have to accept the fact that I was now single and lonely, but I had to email the bride and groom and tell them I would no longer be bringing my former plus-one. Soul crushing. Seriously.

Thankfully, I have kick-ass friends who turned the wedding into a group date. We all piled into the car and made our way to yet another generic wedding venue. Please note: They all become lackluster after you've been to so many—even the wedding I recently attended at the Natural History Museum in Downtown Los Angeles. After you add the flowers, the dresses, the tablecloths, and the sappy emotions, it all becomes indistinguishable. Regardless of the fact that there's a badass *T. rex* hovering over the bride and groom.

On our car ride over, no one mentioned the fact that I was now single. Maybe they were trying not to poke the bear, or maybe this bear was just overly sensitive to the fact that no one was saying anything. I just assumed they felt like they needed to walk on eggshells. Either way, we all carried on as if everything was business as usual. Making inappropriate jokes as we drove, sipping from flasks in the parking lot, and having a heated debate about whether or not "wine and beer only" can be classified as an "open bar." Sure, you don't have to pay, and you can drink as much as you want, but the lack of liquor, in my opinion, disqualifies it from holding the title of "open." I should have been on a debate team.

After the ceremony, which I can't remember because my brain eventually blended them all together, I went to find my table place card. They had been set up on a long cloth, organized by table number, rather than in alphabetical order. My OCD flared. This system didn't make sense to me. Neither does marriage, so "just go with it," I self-soothed.

My eyes scanned the rows of cards, up and down, left to right. Then, there it was. TABLE 9—LISA SCHWARTZ. I picked it up. I took one more glance down to make sure my friends were at that table too, and like that gut-wrenching moment when you discover your first gray hair or that random chin whisker, I saw a card that read TABLE 9—SHANE DAWSON. I reread it. TABLE 9—SHANE DAWSON. As in my ex-boyfriend, my former plus-one? TABLE 9—SHANE

DAWSON. Yep. It was him, all right. My heart dropped into my stomach. I was absolutely mortified.

I ran over to my friends, who were shoving as many appetizers as they could into their mouths, and I practically shouted with tears in my eyes, "They have a fucking place setting for Shane!" I waved the card in front of them as proof.

Their jaws dropped. Impressively, the mini quiches they'd just popped into their mouths didn't. There was silence, then whispers of "holy shit" and "no way." We all took a gulp of our drinks, and then as if rehearsed, we broke into synchronized laugher. Full-blown and uncontrollable. We couldn't stop. We had avoided the subject of my breakup all day. Kept tight-lipped and cautious up to that point. But this place card, this tiny piece of folded cardboard, opened the floodgates. This was literally the cruelest and funniest joke I couldn't have written better if I tried.

Laughing about it with my friends felt so good. It was like I finally took that dump I had been holding in all day. Really, is there anything better? I had been so afraid of burdening them with my crap (poop pun 100 percent intended) that I pretended like I was fine up to this point, when the reality was, I was silently struggling with the fact that I was newly single at a wedding. Yet, with every snort laugh that came out of me, I felt a little lighter in my heart and stronger in my ability to get through the night with my friends by my side.

We sat down at table 9, with one vacant place setting

beside me. The whole table glanced at the empty chair and chuckled at yet another jab at my stag status. I opened my purse and pulled out Shane's place card and carefully displayed it on the empty seat. I'll never pass up embellishing a joke if I can. When the waiter came around and filled our glasses with wine, Randi's husband lifted a glass to make a toast.

"To Shane!" he announced as he swayed his glass toward the empty chair.

Everyone paused and looked at me.

I lifted up my glass, directed it toward the vacant spot, and laughed. "To Shane!"

The rest of the table followed suit. It is one of my most favorite wedding memories.

For the remainder of the party, someone would randomly refer to the missing guest.

"Can you pass me Shane's butter?"

"Is Shane going to drink that water, or can I have it?"

"If Shane's not dancing, I'm not dancing."

Some jokes get old, but this one could have gone on forever. It was hilarious and, more importantly, therapeutic. It was also a reminder that weddings are absurd, and worrying about getting married is even more absurd. So, you might as well embrace where you are now, enjoying your friends that laugh beside you, and cracking jokes about your boyfriend past.

After that night, I didn't hate going to weddings anymore. In fact, Wedding Seven was an absolute blast. Sure, the couple was adorable and the DJ was awesome, but I mostly enjoyed it because I wasn't thinking of weddings as pressured case studies on my personal growth and just enjoyed it for what it was: a celebration of two people making a commitment to making the most of what they got going on together. That's a pretty cool thing.

I'm still not convinced marriage is for me, but I no longer stew over it, because the only place that got me was kneeled over the fancy porta-potty toilet at Wedding Three, after attempting to chug all my worries away. Wait—THAT'S why Wedding Three was a bit of a blur. Not my proudest moment.

I am proud, however, to have made the decision that if I can't be with someone who will bust a move with me—to the point of full-blown sweat—on a wedding dance floor, I will gladly continue to toast the empty chair beside me.

Little Miss Bossy

Here's to those who wish us well, and those who don't can go to hell.

—Elaine Benes

According to sources (my brother), I was a bossy kid growing up. I insisted we do things my way and was unwilling to ever negotiate. If he wanted to hang out with me, we were going to play "school," we were going to use my Cabbage Patch dolls as students, and I was going to be the principal. My brother always had to be the underpaid teacher and report to my office for a review every afternoon. His reviews usually didn't go great and often resulted in a firing. The fact that this didn't deter him from becoming a college professor in his adult life is pretty incredible. I'll go ahead and take credit for his current success.

I have memories of every one of my family members calling me bossy at one point or another. Nowadays, we are lucky enough to live in a society in which the push for female empowerment is at an ultimate high, but back when

I was a kid, speaking up for what I wanted was considered pushy. There was even a book called *Little Miss Bossy* that my parents got for me as a nod to my attitude and a lesson in behavior. I'm sure you've seen this series of books, but for those who haven't, *Little Miss Bossy* is a round, blue cartoon lady who is known for shouting orders and bossing people around. Her boyfriend was Mr. Grumpy and her house resembled a boot camp. None of the other Little Misses and Misters liked Miss Bossy until she vowed to never be bossy again.

I wanted to be liked so badly that I decided, outside of my home, I couldn't be Little Miss Bossy. Now that I think about it, I was suppressing my instincts to be a leader and quieting my authentic voice. Dude, I'm literally making discoveries as I type. Should I call up my one-hundred-year-old grandpa and yell at him for calling me selfish that one time? I can totally hear his response now:

"What? I can't hear you. Do you have a boyfriend yet?"

It wasn't until I entered my thirties that I began to embrace and understand the power of being bossy. That traditionally negative term is actually the key to sustainable happiness. Don't get it twisted—I'm not implying that you have to be a heartless bitch to find joy. I've watched enough teen movies to know that the mean, popular girl isn't actually happy. I've also enjoyed enough teen movies to know that my taste in film is totally embarrassing. I'm just saying I discovered that packing away those parts of me was actually doing me a disservice.

The opposite of bossy is submissive. Unless I am living out some *Fifty Shades of Grey* fantasy, I never want to be compliant. Seriously, I have spent thirty-plus years conforming to the whims of others, and where did that get me? I know—saying yes to everything, even when in my heart I said no. Like that time I agreed to see *Fifty Shades of Grey* with my mother. Huge mistake. I can never get back the two hours spent watching that lackluster soft-core porn. More importantly, I'll never be able to scrub the image of my mom's face when Mr. Grey spanked the shit out of Anastasia. My mother's enthusiasm for that moment is the reason the *Fifty Shades* franchise is booming and I'm in therapy.

Besides avoiding watching socially acceptable porn with your mom, taking on the task of being bossy means fighting for what you want, speaking up against the things you don't want, and delegating tasks that you don't need to take on yourself. All this without worrying what other people are thinking of you.

Throughout most of my twenties, I worked at a dance studio teaching musical theater. This was in conjunction with my million other jobs and the start of my YouTube career. Call me all the names you want, Grandpa, but lazy certainly can't be one of them. I loved that job, passing on my appreciation for the art of jazz hands and vibrato, but I hated the lady I worked for. She was a Southern woman who was not only a closed-minded conservative, but she basked in the glory of her boss status by treating me like utter crap. She is a perfect example of the kind of "bossy" you don't want to aim for. On many occasions, she would unjustly blame me for a complaint the studio would get, "accidentally" leave me off the staff party invites, and completely dismiss me when I had a valid question or concern. I'm still not sure where her disdain for me came from, or why she didn't just fire me if she thought I wasn't doing a good job. I guess she didn't have a viable reason; I always arrived on time and stayed late, exceeded job expectations, and never asked for overtime. I could have written the damn employee manual.

I remember one afternoon the mailman dropped off a large package at the studio that all the staff seemed very excited about. When I went to see what all the fuss was for, I saw that everyone was being given their own box of business cards that had their individual names on them. As silly as a little rectangle seemed, it was thrilling to think that I would have my very own. That small piece of high-quality paper meant that I was doing something important enough to warrant such a thing. I couldn't wait to tell my dad; he would be so proud. When I put my hand out to receive my box, the owner looked at me blankly.

"They must have forgotten yours," she said, with a bunch of unopened boxes in front of her. Any moron would know she was lying; she didn't even look inside the boxes to make sure mine weren't there. If she wasn't going to get me my own cards, the least she could have done was faked it a little better. I was soul crushed and extremely embarrassed. After three years of dedication to the studio, she couldn't have slapped my name on a few cards like everyone else?

"Here," she said, handing me a handful of generic studio cards. "You can write your name on the back."

I grabbed a pen and cowered back to the teachers' break room with a stack of nameless cards and a broken heart. To this day, this story still upsets me. I wish I could go back and hug that timid twenty-seven-year-old who sat for an hour, sadly writing her name on the back of each card. I wish I could have taken that pen and stabbed the stupid, mean boss's eyes out. I wish I would have spoken up for myself and asked her why she felt so comfortable treating me, a fellow woman who was representing her and her company, so poorly.

I stuck with the job awhile longer after that incident because I needed the money, and I refused to let my handmade cards go to waste. In the back of my mind, though, I was plotting out my next move. The card disaster may have been hurtful in the moment, but it was the fuel that finally relit my Little Miss Bossy fire I had suppressed so many years ago. I didn't deserve to be treated like crap. In fact, I didn't deserve to be dismissed by a lady whose last three years of success were a direct result of me and my fellow teachers working at minimum wage for her. Over the course of my time there, she barely even showed up. The only manual labor I knew she was engaging in was shoving money under her mattress. That power play was bullshit. I was mentally drained; it was finally time to make a change.

One night, while sharing a bottle of wine and comparing horror stories from our day of teaching, my friend Laurel and I decided we should start our own studio. We wanted be our own bosses, run our place how we wanted, and be compensated the way we deserved to be. We were hyped by this newfound plan but decided to sleep on it, knowing we often came up with crazy ideas whenever we drank together. We once thought it would be brilliant to make a Christian dance workout video line called Jazz Hands for Jesus. Neither of us are Christian or have any interest in workout videos, but for some reason our Pinot Noir thought otherwise.

We woke up the next day and were 100 percent certain that it was our turn to take the reins and be the boss ladies, so that's what we set out to do. We didn't know the first thing about starting a business but we were committed to figuring it out. We each threw in one hundred dollars from our last paycheck at the studio and shook on a fifty-fifty partnership. We also may have "borrowed" the client list from the Southern boss demon when we left that horrible place for the last time.

Over the course of the next several years, we worked tirelessly to turn this idea into a booming reality. We held classes in "rent by the hour" dance studios that could double as garbage cans. We made costumes for the kids out of our old clothes and begged our friends to help build sets. We crossed our fingers that nothing bad would happen, knowing we couldn't afford insurance. We smiled and pretended like we had a handle on what we were doing but panicked and scrambled to hold it together. We laughed as our classes began to fill to capacity and celebrated when we realized we were expanding at a rapid rate. And right around the time I turned thirty, we cried tears of joy as we stood outside our very own storefront. The power of being bossy was right before our eyes; we had achieved what we set out to do. We had become not only our own bosses but the owners of the most popular children's musical theater program in our town. Also, I finally had a business card with my name on it.

The company ran for seven years. I'd be lying if I said it was always a magical experience. When you are working in customer service, especially relating to children, you have to deal with a lot of not-so-kind people. Being an owner is fantastic, but not when you have to explain to an entitled Beverly Hills mother why we didn't cast her nightmare child as Annie. Not to mention we had to hire teachers to work for us, and the stress of quality controlling them ALMOST made me sympathize with the Southern boss lady. I'd like to think we had far more restraint in terms of abusing our title, but I'm sure there were moments our staff felt otherwise.

Rounding out the seventh year, we decided the company wasn't serving us anymore. We were making money (although we weren't rolling in it, because we actually paid our teachers what they deserved as a nod to our former broke selves in the same positions), but we were no longer finding the joy in it. We were simply going through the motions, focusing on the negatives, and ignoring the other parts of our lives that needed attention. For Laurel, that meant her three gorgeous children, whom she had popped out over the course of our business adventure. For me, it meant putting all of my focus on my YouTube career, which only got half my attention since I started this company.

Closing the doors to our business was one of the hardest but greatest things we could have done. It was beyond difficult to say goodbye to the chapter in our lives that had developed and defined us as strong and independent bossy women. You better believe we obsessively questioned the choice and continuously changed our minds up until the literal moment when I had to hand over our keys. In the end, we were positive that a good boss must not be afraid to make a difficult decision, sticking her neck out for what she needs. Ending this part of our careers gave us that much-needed space to grow both our lives in new directions.

All of this isn't to say you need to be a literal boss to be a "boss." I just was so sick of letting people step all over me, specifically in a work setting, that I wanted to take control of my life. Starting a business was the extreme version of that, but I guess that's what twenty-plus years of holding back got me. I finally gave myself the permission to speak up and be the person I wanted to be, regardless of what other people thought of me. That makes you a boss.

Shortly after closing the company, my YouTube channel started to boom again. It had slowly declined during the last few years of running the studio, so getting back the extra time to focus on it gave it the boost it needed. I was elated and relieved knowing that the energy I had once spent on the studio was more effectively being used on YouTube.

I was at dinner with a group of friends, when someone mentioned how excited they were to see that my channel was growing and how impressed they were that I had been self-employed for all these years. Please note, I HATE talking about work with my friends. It makes me so uncomfortable, and I would literally rather talk about ANYTHING else. What's the most boring subject on the planet? Gas prices? Traffic? Taxes? My friend's kid? Yes, let's talk about those instead.

Regardless of my disdain for chatting about my work, my friends were overly generous with their encouragements and appeared genuinely interested in knowing more. Just when I finally began to open up and feel comfortable with sharing, a member of the group said:

"I just don't GET YouTube."

My heart sank. The minute I allowed myself to be vulnerable and speak up, I was shot down. I don't know why she said that, or if it was meant to be as condescending as it sounded, but the whole group went silent. I can't remember how we U-turned out of that moment and landed in a conversation about raising kids, but I do know I've never been so happy to be talking about breastfeeding than I was right then.

After the dinner, I checked in with Randi and Jessica to make sure I wasn't wrong for feeling so terrible after that comment was thrown at me. Both of them seemed to have been just as taken aback, theorizing it came from a place of jealousy and competitiveness. It's hard to imagine being this way with a friend, but I guess it is naïve of me to think it's not possible. My heart hurt for a long time after that, wondering if the work I do was off-putting to the people around me. It's pretty incredible how one person's hurtful comment can get in your head and affect you so deeply, while the copious number of kind comments from everyone else quickly go forgotten. In that moment, my confidence snatched, I began to obsess about what people thought of me.

My mom always told me to be on the lookout for signs that appear around you, for they are placed there to remind you that you are on the right path. It sounds totally insane to believe that finding a penny on the ground or a feather by your car is some "higher power" reassurance that you're making the right choices, but who am I to be certain otherwise? In moments of desperation, when I feel lost and am questioning my next steps, I always look for a sign.

Not long after the awkward dinner with my friends, I went to see a professional production of *Annie* (sans the obnoxious parents harassing me about their children's involvement). During intermission, I got an email inviting me to meet Hillary Clinton at a Q&A specifically for YouTubers, during her presidential campaign tour. Whether you are a fan of hers or not, it's hard to deny what an incredible and rare opportunity this was. I've never responded yes to an invite so quickly (and I've been invited to a lot of open-bar events)!

On the day of the event, I was riddled with nerves and excitement because I was about to meet the boss lady herself. Never in my wildest dreams did I imagine I would get to meet a former first lady and a future president of the United States. Obviously, my dreams didn't come to full fruition, but I did get to shake Senator Hillary Clinton's hand. I also told her she was fantastic on *Broad City*, to which she replied with a bright smile:

"Oh, thank you. That's a wonderful show."

I figured she needed a little break from the political talk, and her response made me love her even more. It was one of the most memorable days of my life.

That night, I also signed some final paperwork that made me an official first-time homeowner. As I popped a bottle of champagne I had been saving for a special occasion, not thinking it would be THIS special, I had a moment of clarity. I was thirty-three, I bought a house completely on my own, and I got to meet one of the greatest female powerhouses of my generation. This all happened because I decided to take charge and focus on my YouTube career.

Then, there it was—the signs: the invite, the handshake, the homeownership. They may have not been in the form of pennies or feathers, but I would argue that social interaction with Hillary Clinton and keys to a new home were pretty clear signs I was on the right path. I wanted to call up that girl who told me she didn't "GET" YouTube and see if she got it now, but I refrained and posted a picture with me and my best friend, Hillary Clinton, instead.

Finishing up that special-occasion champagne, I reflected on the glory of all the life-changing opportunities that came my way because I had decided, that day in the teachers' break room, while I spent an hour writing my name on the back of the business cards, that I would never allow my career and life to take a backseat again. I was born to be Little Miss Bossy, and I'm never again going to let anyone make me feel otherwise.

From one boss to another:

Cheers to you and your bossy aspirations.

Twelve Whiskeys and a Funeral

I can't die with dignity. I have no dignity. I want to be the one person who doesn't die with dignity. I've lived my whole life in shame! Why should I die with dignity?

—George Costanza

The minute the clock struck midnight and the ball dropped on the TV in the back of the bar, my friends and I hopped into Ubers and headed to our respective homes. We entered 2018 with a passionate urge to be in bed, asleep. When had we become such old people? Actually, that's not a fair assessment of old people; the seniors in my family love the nightlife. Just the other night, my grandma called me out for leaving her favorite jazz bar before 10 p.m.

"You're going home this early?" she said with judgment in her eyes and party in her soul. She's my hero.

Maybe one day I'll make the switch and become a night owl again, but for the time being, my friends and I prefer to start early, to sleep early. If you begin drinking at

5 p.m., you can get in a solid few hours of partying and still be in bed by 10. This may sound lame, but it's efficient as fuck. By 7 a.m., you feel great, and you can start a brand-new fresh day. I should be a health guru, with my lecture circuit, "How to Get the Most Bang for Your Two-Buck Chuck: A Guide to Productive Drinking."

Back on New Year's Eve, I climbed into bed as soon as I got home at 12:25 a.m. on the dot. I was looking forward to my first deep sleep of 2018. My eyes closed, my mind drifted, and I began to nod off. Then a loud ding on my phone yanked me out of my slumber. My heart began to race. (As you will later come to find out, I don't have the greatest experience with middle-of-the-night texts.) I rolled over, alarmed, seeing now that it was 1:30 a.m. and I had a text message from my mom. Shit…shit…shit…It couldn't be good. I swiped open my phone and read the text in a state of panic.

> **Mom:** Lisa. I can't get Uber to work on my phone. Trying to get home from a party. Can you call one for me?

Seriously? My mom is still out partying? Another ding.

> **Mom:** [Bitmoji of her swinging on a heart that says "I love you"]

I don't know if I was more frustrated that I had been woken up with fear, that I had to pay for her ride, or that her stupid Bitmojis looked more like Lady Gaga than her. Whatever the case, I was just glad nothing bad had happened to her. This must have been what it felt like for my parents when I would call them in the middle of the night to get picked up from a slumber party, which was a regular occurrence for me when I was a kid. I don't know why I had such trouble sleeping at other people's houses. Maybe it was an early sign of my social anxiety and my infinite love of hibernating. I wonder, had Uber been around, if my parents would have said, "Just take a damn Uber." Lucky for them, I would have at least known how to use the freaking app. I ordered her the car and stayed up until she texted to say she had gotten home safely. That wasn't the first time I felt like my mom's parent, and it certainly wasn't going to be the last.

Once, when I was really young, maybe five or six, I went into her room to find her sitting on the bed, in full-blown tears, with a round brush tangled tightly in her eighties perm. I asked her what was wrong, and she told me the brush was stuck and she couldn't seem to get it out. I asked why that made her so upset. Besides the obvious reason—having a brush fastened to your skull—her emotions seemed a little blown out of proportion, even to a kid who threw tantrums on a regular basis. My mom explained that she was PMSing, which was the first time I had learned of such a wretched thing. She described it as the time right before a woman gets her monthly "flow," when you feel like utter crap, want to eat the whole pantry, and are simultaneously sad and mad about everything and anything. Maybe this is why I was so freaked out when I first got my period, and why I also have a strong disdain for the term "flow." Every other girl was excited, thinking they were now mature and cool because they were bleeding. Which, ew, *gross*. I never saw the correlation there. I was just terrified, remembering the horrifying warning my mom had instilled in me. The only thing I couldn't wait for was having a proper excuse to devour a sleeve of Oreos in one sitting.

As mom sat there deflated, I hugged her real tight and then began to slowly untangle her hair from the brush, one strand at a time. Her tears dried up, and her fragile state decreased. In that moment, I was taking care of her, without even realizing it.

When I was twelve, my family and I went on a cruise to Mexico. It was something we did a lot, instead of adventurous things like camping or skiing. The Schwartzes are not outdoor people. My family preferred the routine and comfort of doing the same thing every year. All-inclusive, all scheduled, all in one place, 100 percent OCD friendly. The details of that trip are now a little vague to me, but I do remember a particular conversation I had with my mom in the hot tub like it was yesterday. My parents had been fighting the whole trip, which wasn't anything new, but something must have pushed her over the edge. Sitting in a pool of steaming chlorine with chubby twelve-year-old me wearing a bathing suit with an extra-large T-shirt over it, my mom blurted out what felt like a cry for help.

"I can't do it anymore. Lisa, I just can't do it anymore."

I wasn't exactly sure what that meant, or why she decided to share this with me—it's not like I had any mature insight or life experience at that point. The only thing I was an expert on was bread rolls and the fact that I could shove two of them in my mouth at once. Looking back, talking about relationship issues with your pre-teen daughter seems like an inappropriate parent move. Although, I understand that uncontrollable human need to get out your feelings after holding them in for so long. She was a human in pain who needed an outlet, a friend, someone to talk to. For better or for worse, that person was me. It pained me, seeing her hurt, knowing I couldn't make it better. All I could think to do was wrap my arms around her and float with her in silence.

In that moment, it sunk in that my mom was just a human like everyone else. She wasn't a superhero or the invincible robot that I once wanted to believe she was. She had flaws and problems like I did, and now I was privy to them. Remember that mind-blowing feeling you had when you saw your teacher outside of school for the first time? "How could that possibly be?" you thought to your five-year-old self. "You mean to tell me Ms. Fruend is allowed out and isn't always in business-casual attire? Wait—she has a first name and a family? You have got to be fucking kidding me!" Yeah, that is what this felt like.

Something I feel like no one ever warns you about is that as you get older, the parent-child roles start to do these Freaky Friday–type switches. With every switched experience comes an emotional awareness that your parents are getting older and will have to rely on you more and more. This is not only a melancholy realization to come to, acknowledging they aren't going to be around forever, but it's also a jarringly stressful concept, figuring out how you are going to take care of them in the future.

I actually had a psychic tell me once that I was my mom's mom in a past life. She also told me that I was meant to be in politics. To be fair, politicians are some of the best actors, so I'm going to let that one slide. What I wish she would have told me was that in my current life, I would have to step up and take care of my mom under one of the worst circumstances any child could imagine. Maybe I should have asked the psychic lady for my money back.

Right around the time I turned thirty, I was forcefully catapulted back into the position of my mom's parent. The smaller moments from my childhood paled in comparison to what I was unknowingly entering into. Mom had been dating a man by the name of Rodger for about two years. He came after the creepy hoarder guy but before the butt-grabbing drunk guy. My mom admittedly doesn't have the best taste, but Rodger was different than the others. Rodger was kind and humble. Simple and stylish. Sweet and intelligent. A delightful departure from my mom's usual less-than-refined palate.

Unless I'd had a few too many to drink, I didn't keep my ringer on at night. I am an unpleasant creature if I don't get a solid ten-plus hours of sleep, which I realize is an excessive amount, but that's how my pain-in-the-ass self functions. If I had my way, I'd be going to bed at nine every night. I once dated a guy who was so irked by my sleep schedule that he angrily shouted during one of our fights, "You're not living an age-appropriate lifestyle!" I still don't know if he was comparing me to a baby or to an elderly person. All I knew was that he was a dick, so I broke up with him and went to bed at nine.

Anyway, I was fast asleep when I suddenly woke up with a sense of urgency. It was the middle of the night, and I wasn't even halfway to my ten-hour goal. Something told me I needed to check my phone (maybe it was the sixth sense I'm positive I have). I know it's irrational, but so many times I've been randomly thinking about some-one and then, within minutes, they will call. Or a song will pop in my head, and shortly after, that song will come on the radio. Maybe that's a bad example; they play the same four songs on the radio each and every day. The chances of that Drake song stuck in my head coming on are pretty good. Also, I don't listen to Drake. I was just trying to sound hip and relatable. If I made a reference to some oldies song that they always play on the oldies station, I'd sound like an oldie myself. Shit, that dick I was dating may have been right about me.

The glow from my phone screen felt harsh to my sleepy eyes, so I squinted to read the text message that had been awaiting me. It was from my mom, sent at 1:30 a.m.

Mom: Lisa. 911.

My heart dropped into my stomach / beat out of my chest / any other hyperbolic explanation for a feeling just short of a heart attack. I immediately dialed her number, holding my breath without realizing it until she picked up.

A weeping shell of my mother answered the phone. Her words were scrambled, but I could piece together the basic facts. Rodger was dead. He died right in front of her. She left his house after the paramedics came and was back at her apartment now. She was not ok.

Before she could even hang up, I was in the car, headed over to her house. It was pitch-dark outside when I pulled into the driveway. I remember it being surprisingly cold for a spring night in Los Angeles, or maybe I was just chilled by the reality of the situation. I knocked on my mom's back door. She cracked it open, forgetting to unhook the chain lock that had once been installed to make her feel safe. Through the sliver of the opened door, I could see her mortified and depleted soul.

When she finally unhooked the chain, she fell into my arms. A move I had done so many times with her, after a breakup or a bad audition. All those things that had seemed so detrimental to me at the time were meaningless compared to what was happening to her now. My mom wept into my neck, filling the crevices of my collarbone with her horrified tears. I listened as she replayed the night over and over again. Each time, she would retell it in muttered segments, never actually stringing a full sentence together. After the third or fourth time she nonsensically circled around the story, I convinced her to get into bed.

The sun would rise soon, and I knew she had a few long days ahead of her. I laid her down, like she used to do with me so many years ago, climbing in with her, and wrapping my arms around her as tightly as I could. I wanted to take the hurt away, give her back the piece of her heart that was so aggressively ripped from her. I rubbed her back until her staccato breaths deepened and slowed themselves down. Finally, I was watching her sleep, piecing together what had actually happened to this broken woman in my arms. Rodger had died while making love to her. That's more information than I ever needed to know, and more pain than I ever wanted her to feel.

As I lay there watching Mom sleep, I felt sick with fear, knowing I was ill equipped to handle this situation. I like to think I have good instincts, but nothing can prepare a child for this kind of responsibility. I knew I was going to have to step up and be the parent she needed, like the one she had always been to me, even if I wasn't exactly sure how. My mom had always unselfishly put her issues aside, time and time again, to be my support system whenever I needed it. From seemingly small things like dropping everything she was doing to come bring me a spare key because I locked myself out of my apartment for the fiftieth time, to holding me on multiple occasions as I rocked back and forth on my bedroom floor in an unwavering panic attack, my mom would stop at nothing to make sure I was safe, loved, and taken care of. She has always been my rock and would go to any lengths to make sure I felt that. It was my turn to be hers, because she had lost all the strength she had the minute she realized Rodger wasn't breathing. I was going to figure out how to take care of her—I had no other choice.

The day of the funeral, I put on a black dress and picked up my mother to take her to the cemetery. My brother wasn't able to fly home from his job in Florida, so I had the task of carrying her through the day. She looked gorgeous, despite the drab circumstances. She wore a black velvet dress, matching black gloves, and a black hat clad with a piece of sheer fabric dangling just low enough to cover her swollen eyes. She looked like something out of a movie, a glamorous widow from a more romantic time period. I wondered what she thought about when she was getting ready that morning. Was she purposefully trying to look extra put together, hoping the others attending wouldn't notice just how much she was crumbling inside? Or was she not thinking at all, just shifting into autopilot, as she perfectly curled each strand of her gray-rooted blonde hair?

The ceremony was held in a Catholic church, located in the middle of the cemetery. I don't recall much from the actual mass, just the constant kneeling, tissue passing, and the look on my mom's face whenever her name was mentioned. A mixed expression of honor, pride, sorrow, and hollowness. After a drawn-out combination of prayers and sermons, Rodger's son got up to speak. He was a former child actor turned rap star wannabe. I couldn't make this up if I tried. He embodied every stereotype you would assume of a Hollywood-raised child—G-Wagon and hot supermodel girlfriend to boot.

"My dad went out doing the thing he loved," he

announced to the pews of horrified mourners, including my mother. For someone aspiring to be a master of words, he certainly lacked an ability to put the tasteful ones together. I'm going to let him off the hook this time— everyone grieves differently. I wonder if Eminem is also terrible at giving funeral speeches.

After the ceremony, we headed to that son's less-than-humble abode in the Hollywood Hills. The backyard was filled with long banquet tables holding copious amounts of Italian food and endless bottles of wine and high-end liquor. Music blared from the large stereo system, which was attached to the largest TV screen I had ever seen. I was accustomed to "sitting shiva," which involves deli platters, quiet small talk, and the stench of antiques and plastic-covered furniture. This here was a downright celebration. An excuse to drink and eat and blow off steam. And that's exactly what we did.

From this point on, my memory of the night plays in segments. Like an old picture slideshow that momentarily goes black with the sound of the shutter before the next picture appears.

Mom and I eating pasta, even though we hadn't felt the sensation of hunger since the night Rodger died.

Black. Shutter.

Mom and I drinking whiskey. Neither of us whiskey drinkers, but not thinking twice about our choice.

Black. Shutter.

Mom looking into my eyes, telling me she's not ok without having to say a word. I hold her hand.

Black. Shutter.

Mom and I drinking another glass of whiskey. Neither of us taking a beat to enjoy it. Just racing to get it down.

Black. Shutter.

Mom and I in the bathroom. She is looking at her sunken eyes in the mirror. I flush the toilet and tell her she still looks gorgeous.

Black. Shutter.

Mom dancing with an attractive friend of the rap wannabe. He is coked out of his mind. She's smiling for the first time in a long time. I see a glimpse of her former joy.

Black. Shutter.

Mom and I smoking a joint. I am tripping out that we're doing this, that she's doing this. I'm not sure it's actually happening.

Black. Shutter.

Mom and I laughing hysterically. Then we are crying. Then we are cry laughing.

Black. Shutter.

Mom and I taking a shot of whiskey.

Black. Shutter.

Mom and I dancing to a Prince song. We are drenched in our own sweat. We can't stop dancing. We finally feel nothing.

Black. Shutter.

Me telling my mom I love her, that I will always protect her. I hold her hand.

Black. Shutter.

Waking up the next morning, still in my funeral dress, with mascara running down my face.

A text from my mom. Shit…shit…shit…

> **Mom:** Thank you for taking care of me last night. I don't remember most of it. I just remember dancing with you. And you, holding my hand, taking away the pain.

No Bitmoji, no requests for help, no bad news. I had accomplished what I so desperately set out to do. Even if it was just for that one night, I was the rock that protected my mother, and there was no greater feeling.

I'm now aware, as I get older, that there will be more moments when I'll need to step into their parenting shoes, even if I don't feel fully equipped to do so. As scary as the thought of that is, there is something quite beautiful about it. It's the circle of life—straight-up, baby-Simba-being-lifted-into-the-air life.

This shift in the family dynamic is bound to happen to all of us at some point. In fact, I'm acutely aware of how fortunate I am to still have both of my parents to care for. Even if my mom drives me nuts with her inability to use technology or accurately portray herself in cartoon form. In those frustrating moments, when I want to pull out my hair because she calls to ask me how her printer works for the millionth time, I remind myself of that night I held her in my arms. I remember how desperately I wanted to make all of her pain go away, how badly I wanted to take care of her the way she's always taken care of me. Now I will finally have the opportunity to slowly pay her back, the best I know how. From experience, I can say sweating whiskey from dancing too hard to Prince with your beautiful mother is not a bad start.

My Four-Legged Child

Dogs are the leaders of the planet. If you see two life forms, one of them's making a poop, the other one's carrying it for him, who would you assume is in charge?

—Jerry Seinfeld

I'm not sure if I want to have a baby. I don't really have an instinctive feeling one way or another. Thankfully I don't have a partner eager to knock me up (one perk of being single). I do, however, have a voice inside my head, crafted by the whispers of societal standards, reminding me I'm getting kind of old for baby making. Not, like, the sexy part—you're never too old for that, thanks to modern medication (#notsponsored by Viagra). Just the part where I'm too old for the literal bearing of a child. According to the internet, which is always 100 percent accurate, women thirty-five and older who are with child are considered a geriatric pregnancy. By that criteria, if and when I get knocked up, I will be a GERIATRIC pregnant bitch.

I added "bitch" because I anticipate being a complete nightmare.

My therapist suggested I make a pros and cons list to help me sort out the whole baby thing, after I mentioned I felt like I was getting a little old to not have a strong opinion on it. When I sat down to write the list, I only came up with one reasonable reason why I should have a baby—to ensure I have someone to take care of me when I'm old and need a sponge bath. Although I hope I'm rich enough that I can hire a super-hot young dude to do it. I guess I could have come up with more pros, but I figured if I left it at just that, I could justify not freezing my eggs, as has been suggested on a loop for the past few years. With that, my list of cons flowed a lot easier.

*Please note: These are dramatic assumptions. You are probably a perfect parent and none of these apply to you. So, screw you. Also, I totally want to be you.

MY HAVING-A-BABY CONS

- Being pregnant destroys your body. Selfish, I realize, but I'm already so hard on myself. I can't imagine trying to lose the baby weight after nine months of shoving French fries in my face without having a complete meltdown. Yes, I know you don't have to eat French fries while pregnant, but I will. It's nonnegotiable.
- You're always tired. Not because you were out partying or doing something fun. Simply because your baby wakes up, crying, every hour on the hour. This

continues until the baby is awake for the day, and you feel like utter death.

- You never have sex with your significant other after you have your baby. You're exhausted, don't have time, and you're embarrassed that your vagina is now a large mess.

- Most importantly—and my biggest deterrent to having a baby—you don't love your dog anymore. Argue all you want, but the majority of women I know who loved their dogs so much prebaby could easily do without them postbaby. This is devastating and heart-breaking and I refuse to accept this as my future.

According to greeting cards and trinkets you find at the carwash, dogs are man's best friend. This is totally sexist and doesn't do justice to the depth of the relationship. No offense to my best friends, but my dog is more than that. A dog is a single woman's other half, ride or die, copilot, and hairy guardian angel. My pup has been with me through some of my most private and emotional times, and I swear that little beast understands.

So, until I can be convinced otherwise, I choose my pup over pregnancy. She's like having a child anyway, but I can leave her home alone and not worry that she might stick her fingers in the electrical socket or find my porn. What more could you ask for?

Recently, I was driving just to drive, windows down, a Sara Bareilles song blasting, crying because…oh, who knows why this time (I'm a sensitive lady). Whatever the reason, as the tears fell down my cheek, my dog took it upon herself to stand with her paws on the center console and lick them away. As cheesy and dramatic as that sounds—because, yes, I always use Sara Bareilles songs as a therapeutic tool—this moment is one of my most cherished. An emotional sliver in time, shared exclusively with this tiny soul in a fur coat. Sure, my tears are delicious, but I'm certain she was trying to take away my pain in that very moment. It worked. I leaned over and kissed her little face and said, "Thank you." Yes, I talk to my dog. No, that's not the extent of our strange relationship.

This dog came into my life in December of 2012. Shane, my future ex-boyfriend, and I had been going to charity-run dog adoptions every Saturday. We also went to open houses on Sundays, but that's not pertinent to this story. Although maybe we ultimately decided to get a dog so we wouldn't have to commit to getting a house.

One weekend, Shane begged me to go to the city pound. Back then, a majority of the pounds would euthanize the animals if they didn't get adopted, so I avoided going because I was afraid my heart couldn't handle the heartbreak of not being able to save them all. Up until this point Shane and I had only been going to rescue centers set up in the park or outside grocery stores. For some reason Gelson's Market always had them. Come for tuna, leave with a terrier. Makes perfect sense. This weekend, Shane seemed so set on taking our adoption addiction to the next level. Who was I to deny him that pleasure? When we pulled up, he mentioned this particular pound was one of the nicer ones. Why he was an expert on the subject, I'm still not sure, but my anxiety was momentarily eased. We pushed through giant double glass doors that had once been automated and stepped into the large, sterile room. To the right were hundreds of cats in cages, to the left stood an ominous archway to the dogs, and straight ahead was a window where you could conduct business with the emotionless man behind the glass. The space smelled of feces, bleach, and heartbreak.

I looked at Shane nervously. Knowing he was going to have to be the brave one, he grabbed my hand to keep me calm. Together we took a deep breath and headed toward the dog wing. Before we could take more than two steps, a siren went off. It was a shock to my system, like the sound of a fire alarm blaring in a hotel room just hours after you've passed out in a room service–induced food coma. Oddly enough, this has happened to me more than once. Always in New York, always a false alarm, and always when I'm sleeping naked. Talk about an adrenaline rush. This time at the pound felt different. Probably because I was wearing clothes and had a strong premonition that something bad was actually going to happen. A wave of panic set in, and I didn't even know why. We both froze, not sure if we should drop and cover, stand in a doorway, or get the hell out of there. Before we had a chance to make a decision, the large glass doors we had just entered through flung open. In came a gust of wind, two uniformed men, a squeaky gurney, and one very dead-looking dog. I whipped my head away, as soon as I was able to process what I had just seen. I must have turned ghostly white, because Shane looked at me and grabbed my shoulders to make sure I wasn't going to faint. Once the gurney of bloody fur exited into some mysterious hallway, I turned to Shane, and without saying a word, we left.

That was the one and only time I visited the pound. After the initial shock and nausea wore off, we had a good laugh about it. Not about the dead dog—we aren't monsters—just that I had finally given in to the idea of going to a pound and was quickly greeted with the most traumatic experience ever. Needless to say, after that we stuck to adoption centers set up by foundations that visit the pound for you. Not only are they doing a great service to all the animals in need of homes, but they are also serving unstable humans trying to avoid further emotional scarring. I'm a big fan of that cause.

There was a small storefront near our apartment that looked like a pet shop but was run by a nonprofit that housed shelter dogs in need of homes. The local neighborhood kids would volunteer and walk the dogs, while others would pop in and snuggle with them. It was set up to be a sanctuary for dogs and humans alike. Ironically, a few years after I got my dog from there, the place started to go under. I'm not exactly sure what sort of shady shit was going down, but I had gone in there to buy some treats and peruse the newcomers, when I mentioned to an employee that I had gotten my pup when they first opened. She responded by asking, I shit you not, "Is it still alive?" I was so taken aback, and sure that I had misheard her, that I didn't respond. I quickly paid for the treats and left. I was with Jessica when this all went down, so I checked in after to see if she heard the same thing. Sure enough, she heard, "Is it still alive?" as clear as day. That's a saying, right? LA days are so smoggy I've never actually used it. Whatever. That employee's casual tone was unnerving, and thankfully the shop closed a few months later.

Years before the downfall of this community dog haven, Shane and I fell in love with a tiny little puppy with the perfect pink nose. Khloe, formerly named Piggly Wiggly, was a mutt of dachshund, chihuahua, and some other stinking cute descent. Born in a shelter, she had been transported to the store a little too soon after her birth. It didn't seem to dampen her spirit, though. She was a favorite amongst the employees and to the regulars who frequented for a quick burst of dopamine. We must have visited her every day for a solid week before realizing if we didn't take her, someone else would. Because I'm me, and I need to overthink everything, I had a hard time deciding whether or not we should do it. I knew that it was a huge responsibility and would require a lot of work. Shane, on the other hand, seemed so confident that we could handle it that I made him a deal. We were headed to New York the week before Christmas. If we got back and she was still there, we would get her.

On the last night of our trip, I had a moment of clarity and I shouted, "We have to get her!"

Who knows why I all of a sudden felt so certain, but I

went with it. Shane dialed the store as fast as he could and put a deposit down on her over the phone.

The day after Christmas, we walked out of the store as new parents with the most precious bundle of love. I didn't realize it then, but this little dog would end up being the most important partner I've ever had. On the way home, we decided we had to rename her. Khloe was the name of a Kardashian, not our dog. Without thinking, I said, "We should name her Unicorn. Because she's magical."

"Yeah. And we can call her Corny," Shane said without hesitation.

Just two grown-ass adults with one newborn puppy, picking out names like full-on kindergartners.

Unicorn "Corny" Dawson it was, until a year into her life when we decided to change her last name to Schwartz. Separation is a bitch, even for doggy parents. The intention was to have her split time between homes, but Shane quickly realized he wasn't cut out for single fatherhood. Which left me with no choice but to take on the title of single mom. To be clear, Shane pays alimony in the form of the doggy daycare bill, which is so generous and helpful. But ultimately, I had to learn how to take care of a living, breathing, tiny life, all on my own. Guys, I can barely keep a plant alive. This is not an exaggeration. I have been known to kill succulents, and those are damn near impossible to kill. I guess I can be proud that I accomplished the impossible, but when I thought about how that translated to my ability to take care of a dog, I started to worry, and water my plants obsessively.

As luck and common sense would have it, Corny is still alive and well. In fact, after Shane moved out, she transformed into a little human. This is not a punch line; this is the honest truth. Something about the shift in the home dynamic made her so much more aware of me and her place in my life. She became super protective, as evidenced by her habit of insanely barking at people on walks, to the point where I have to make a cute joke so they don't report her to animal control. I have a handful of go-to lines:

"It's just her version of hello!"

"How's that for a wake-up call? Good morning!"

"She hasn't had her coffee yet."

If all else fails, "I'm sorry. She's a real dick." The old lady across the street loves that one.

Corny is also peculiar with men. Whenever I have a gentleman suitor over, she plays hard to get. At first, she barks and cowers in terror, but within ten minutes, she is totally in love. Sitting on their lap, holding unbreakable eye contact, and seeking attention with a constant paw to their chest. She won't stop, even after a proper rub. She demands their attention until the moment they leave, or until I close my bedroom door. I'm a little ashamed to admit this, but she knows when I say, "I'll be right back," that she has to wait outside the bedroom door while mommy and her date do adult stuff. As soon as I'm done, I open the door, and she's there, waiting patiently. I like to think she's proud of my accomplishments, but most likely she's just hopeful I've landed her a new daddy. Poor kid, little does she know it's never going to happen. Mommy has commitment issues.

It's her habits and rituals that make me think Corny is a little human in disguise. We spend so much time together that she has taken to my daily routines. I'm a creature of habit, so I have a sequence I follow in the morning and at night. We all do, right? Or am I a predictable human who has now passed along her OCD to her dog? Don't answer that.

For example, after we both have dinner, Corny lies on my lap and we watch TV. Seriously, she watches with me. Her eyes focus on the screen and that bitch watches *The Bachelor*. If any animal makes an appearance on the screen, she pops up, the hair on her back standing at attention, and she barks like a German shepherd on steroids and Red Bull. Animal Planet is strictly prohibited in our household.

After our unhealthy dose of reality TV, I ask her if she wants to "go pee pee outside, not inside." Why I feel the need to clarify every time, I don't know, but she knows what it means, because she runs to her leash and literally steps into her harness. My dog knows how to dress herself! Is this brilliant or terrifying?

When we get back inside, I turn off the lights, set the alarm, and head to the kitchen to fill up a glass of water. As soon as she sees me do this, she looks right at me, waiting for the sign. I give her a nod, and before I'm even done, she beelines to the bed. I've never met anyone who gets more excited to go to sleep. When I get to my room, I always find her smack in the middle of the king-size bed. I have to gently push her over, climb in, and then watch as she inches closer to my face. I ask, "Can I have a kiss?" She gives me one, because she speaks English, and then she crawls under the covers and curls up right against me. We sleep through the entire night in that position. All of this, the whole night routine, happens again the next night. And the next. And the next.

In case you aren't sold on the fact that my dog is a human, let's play a little game. It's one I like to call Human or Dog. In this game, you will read the prompt and check the box that correlates with the one I'm talking about. The human being me, and the dog being Corny.

Let's begin.

HUMAN or DOG

-Is motivated by food.   ( )   ( )

-Doesn't like the neighbors in #105.   ( )   ( )

-Loves to eat breakfast, then go back to
  sleep.   ( )   ( )

-Prefers to sleep naked.   ( )   ( )

-Isn't a huge fan of washing their hair.   ( )   ( )

-Poops only in the morning, rarely at
  night.   ( )   ( )

-Is better one-on-one than in large
  groups.   ( )   ( )

-Could stand to lose a couple of pounds.   ( )   ( )

-Is good at running but usually walks.   ( )   ( )

-Can't sleep if things aren't in their
  place.   ( )   ( )

Got your answers? Unless you chose both for all of them, you are incorrect. I'm sorry, that entire quiz was a massive trick. I should never be a teacher. I wanted you to clearly see that Corny and I have melded into the same weird person. How did this happen?

I live in an apartment, but surrounding it is a lovely residential neighborhood filled with big, gorgeous homes with big, sparkling-clean windows that I like to look through. Mostly to see how the homes are decorated, but sometimes in the hopes of catching a glimpse of something scandalous going on inside. They all have large, luscious front yards with fancy flowers and kitschy garden signs that Corny loves to poop in front of. On our daily walks, we frequently stroll by this one dream home and its side gate, clad with a gold-plated BEWARE OF DOG sign. Neither of us pay any mind to it, because we are badasses and everyone should beware of us. Just kidding—we are weenies who live in fear. But there has never been any barking behind that gate to indicate pending trouble, and besides, we have no plans of trying to enter. We're nosey, but not criminals.

One day, we were walking by that gate, as we always do, when suddenly we heard barking. I was pleasantly surprised, confirming these people weren't using a fake sign as a deterrent. Not only were they successful folks, with their fancy mansion and all, but they were honest ones. Quickly the barking grew louder and was accompanied by the sound of paws on pavement. Before I could put two and two together, a beast in the form of a shih tzu shot out from behind the gate and came charging at Corny.

Like two drunken, trashy girls going at each other at 2 a.m. outside a nightclub, the dogs began to fight. Full-blown, teeth-out, growls-activated, I'm-going-to-watch-one-eat-the-other kind of fight. Then, something happened to me. Something that I didn't even know could happen to me. Like Bruce Banner exploding into the Hulk, my maternal instincts took over and I became Super "Don't Fuck with My Kid" Mom. I screamed at the top of my lungs as I muscled Corny's leash in the air, swinging her away from danger, all the while kicking the shit out of the shih tzu from hell. Animal activists, have no fear. I wasn't kicking it to hurt it, just to initially unclench its jaw from Corny's neck. You can't put your hands in the mix, or you will no longer have fingers—thus, feet become your only option.

After what felt like hours, the owner of the house came out. At this point, Corny was hiding under a parked car, and I was sweating tears and crying sweat. The lady, draped in pearls, asked what had happened, and I said her dog had gotten out and attacked my dog. She nonchalantly explained that they had been meaning to get the gate fixed and her dog was usually pretty friendly. I don't know if she was overly mellowed out by the fancy white wine these kinds of ladies drink or what, but I grabbed my dog and got the hell out of there. In retrospect, I wish I would have shouted, "I know where you live!" as I walked away. That would have been pretty epic. Instead I held Corny in my arms, still in a full state of panic, kissing her and making sure she was ok. Lucky for us both, she was unscathed. After she shook out, which is a dog's literal way of "shaking it off," she seemed unfazed by it all. I, on the other hand, couldn't shake it off. I was visibly rattled and considered going back to demand some of that fancy white wine. Instead I drank my three-dollar Trader Joe's wine and neurotically watched the dog all night to make sure she didn't show any signs of pain or internal injury.

What I learned from this horrid event is that I do, in fact, have a maternal instinct. I would do anything to keep my baby safe. I feel confident that I would succeed, or at least come out with little to no damage. Whenever we walk by the scene of the crime now, I always hold the leash a little tighter. I didn't think Corny had any memory of it, until recently when we heard a bark from behind the gate and she instantly pulled herself away. She remembers. I hate that she remembers. I never want her to be afraid or hurt. I'm her mom, and I love her so damn much.

Don't get too excited. Just because I know I could be a good mom doesn't mean I'm confident I *want* to be one. It just gives me a little comfort knowing that it's a viable option. In the meantime, I'm going to cherish my time without a kid. At this point, if the love I have for my dog is any indication of what it would be like to have a child, then I'm pretty sure child services would be called. You can't make out with a child, sleep butt to butt with it, and let it watch you have drunk sex with strangers, right? Oh yeah, sometimes I forget to make her wait outside the bedroom door. I'll leave you with that.

Selfish Care: A Guide to Staying Young at Heart and Looking Damn Good While Doing It

Why can't some things be just for me? Is that so selfish?
> —George Costanza

Actually, that's the definition of selfish.
> —Jerry Seinfeld

I was messaging with this dude on a dating app who was baffled when I told him I was spending a week alone at a spa in Arizona.

> You aren't going to take anyone with you?

> Nope. Just need some time to myself.

> A whole week getting massages and facials in the desert?

> Yeah. Also, meditating, doing yoga, and reading.

> That's very LA of you.

What's that supposed to mean?

Seems a little crazy to spend all that time and money on that.

Seems a little crazy that you'd care how I spend my time and money.

I couldn't care less, I'm just not into selfish girls.

Not sure how taking care of my mind and body is selfish, but I hope you find whatever you're looking for. Also, I'm a woman, not a girl. Namaste, bitch.

I probably didn't need to add "bitch" to the end of that, but he had me fired up. What right does this bozo have to make a judgment call about me? Better yet, how wrong is he to assume that self-care is a selfish act? Also, the trip was free because I was doing a promotional YouTube video for the resort, but I wasn't about to tell the bastard that.

Going on that trip alone was one of the greatest things I've ever done. It was invaluable to have the opportunity to sit alone with my thoughts for an extended period of time. The number of creative ideas it sparked, problems I solved, and self-realizations that came to life was priceless. Plus, I didn't have to share my bottle of wine with anyone and I got my body rubbed by a stranger who didn't expect me to call him the next day. If this is selfish, I don't want to be anything but!

It's hard to deny (thanks, internet-dating dude for the reminder) that there's a stigma associated with self-care luxuries, like getting facials or taking Pilates classes—people who engage in them must surely be vapid, vain, and spoiled. I blame a lot of this on reality shows for presenting us with extreme examples. Trust me, you don't have to visit a high-end Kardashian hair salon or make time to get weekly Housewives colonics to properly care for yourself. Although, I did make an appointment to get a colonic once but canceled last minute when it finally sunk in that someone would literally be suctioning the shit out of me. I love a good poop, but I'm fine with doing it without the vacuum up my ass.

The actual reality is there are reasonable things that you can do to treat your body right and to give it a chance at running a little smoother and longer. Yes, humans are like cars. We need to be washed, tuned up, and spoken to with kindness. You've never whispered sweet nothings to your car as you shifted into neutral gear, hoping you'll make it to the gas station on an empty tank? No? Just me? I guess we aren't all irresponsible morons.

I'd like to thank my mother for being my self-care guru. I couldn't have been more than five or six when she started to instill in me the idea that if you take care of yourself early on, you won't look or feel like an old lady by the time you turn thirty. Was she trying to live through me by urging me to wear a bra, way before it was necessary, so as to avoid the drooping boobs she was now dealing with? Did she look in the mirror at her self-proclaimed imperfections and note all the mistakes she had made so that she could encourage me to do otherwise? Was she inappropriately projecting her insecurities on me, a five-year-old whose only real concern was whether to roll or flick her boogers? (Answer: roll then flick. Solid combo.) Probably, but I'll take that over a mom wanting to relive her youth as a beauty pageant queen, forcing her kid into promiscuous child wear.

(Yes, someone is manufacturing those sequined mini stripper clothes for these poor children, and they are making a killing. No judgment from me—I legitimately had a moment, broke in my twenties, when I considered moving to Middle of Nowhere, America, to become a pageant coach. I've watched enough *Toddlers & Tiaras* to know that (1) it is an incredibly profitable industry, and (2) I could absolutely fake it and, in fact, be great at it. I'm certain I could make kids spin in circles and pose for a crowd of weirdoes. All you need is a bag of Skittles for bribing and an empty soul for exploiting. I've already got one; the other I can grab at the gas station.)

Pageant life wasn't in my cards, though. Instead, I was given the life of neurotic self-care thanks to my mother's dire warnings. Wear hats in the summer to avoid skin damage. Wear sunglasses while outside to avoid eye damage. Use earplugs at concerts to avoid ear damage. Don't wear underwear when you sleep to avoid…vagina damage? I'm not sure why she pushed this one so hard on me. She continually told me I had to "air it out" at night. I always did, terrified that my vagina might fall off.

She may have been a bit extreme, but for the most part, I

ended up coming out on top. In fact, so far, I've dodged the old-lady leather skin, and I can hear every single thing the people in the apartment next to me are saying. Probably more a reflection of our thin walls, rather than my acute hearing, but I'll take it as a win. My neighbor and his girlfriend also seem to be "winning" every night until the wee hours. Thanks to my mom's warnings, I have earplugs to get through this nightly concert. Mother knows best, and she reminds me of it whenever the bill comes to the table after a meal.

"I wish I had known how to take care of my skin at such a young age like I taught you. You're welcome. And thank you," she's been known to say while cheekily pushing the check toward me. Works every time.

It would be selfish (correct usage), at this point, for me not to share with you my mom's foolproof plan for aging gracefully. Some of which has been mentioned but will now be conveniently placed in one list for you to refer to when needed. For those who require her credits for validity, Jennifer Schwartz is in her late sixties but looks like she's in her forties. She hasn't had any "work done" but works hard on her mind, body, and spirit. She turns heads when she walks into a room, not only because she's fucking adorable, but because she beams with joy and sparkles with positive energy. She's beautiful inside and out, and I would be happy just having a piece of what she's got going on. She also has a five-star customer rating on Uber and Airbnb, but that's just an added bonus.

Without further ado, I give you:

JEN SCHWARTZ'S LOVE-YOUR-SELF CARE:
A Guide to Staying Young at Heart and
Looking Damn Good While Doing It

1. Drink lots of water. Vodka soda doesn't count.

That's not to say don't drink vodka sodas—my mom
LOVES a vodka soda—she's just adamant about drinking
tons of water throughout the day to keep your skin looking fresh and hydrated. She also told me, "Don't drink
and puke," when I turned twenty-one, which wasn't the
most detailed advice but got me through my birthday
celebration without puking up my blue drinks from TGI
Fridays. Why I was drinking blue drinks and celebrating
my twenty-first at TGI Fridays is a whole other issue my
mom should have warned me about.

2. Floss your teeth. Dental work is expensive.

This is no joke. I didn't realize, until I had to start paying for things on my own, just how expensive avoiding
having all your teeth fall out is. No shade on folks without
teeth, but I prefer to chew my food. I floss every night.

3. Exercise at least three times a week. You're not going to stop your arms from looking like bat wings, but you'll slow down the process.

Other terms for flabby arms include aunty arms, bingo
wings, Hadassah arms, goodbye muscle, and possibly the

most horrible one, widow's curtains. This is terrible and everyone has beautiful arms, but I work out five to six days a week. I also have a sincere fear of bats.

4. Never fall asleep with your makeup on. Your skin will suffer and you will look quite scary in the morning.

I know you want to look pretty "the morning after," but your makeup can't help but smear, turning you into a zombie by the time you wake up. Not to mention your skin under all that makeup is suffocating and slowly dying. You're far better off washing your face and avoiding the dead zombie skin. Unless you're into that sort of thing.

5. Go to therapy. Talking about yourself is acceptable when you're paying for it.

No self-care program would be complete if you didn't address the mental and emotional aspects of your life. You MUST make time for some mental TLC. What's the point of spending all that time doing things like oil pulling to make your teeth white if you don't have the mental willpower to squeak out a smile? Maybe that's a bad example. Who in their right mind feels like they have a right mind after swishing coconut oil in their mouth for twenty minutes? The thought alone makes me want to vomit. Not only does it sound disgusting, but also the idea that you would choose this method over just being a normal person and popping a Crest strip on makes me crazy. I'm all about trying to reduce your intake of chemicals and GMOs and whatever other acronyms are bad for you, but sometimes, you got to just shut off your neurotic brain and pop on a whitening strip. Or better yet, just rock out with your yellow teeth. My teeth are a direct reflection of my devotion to coffee and red wine. You may think they are disgusting, but my favorite liquids are beyond flattered.

6. Eat your veggies but have a bite of the cake once in a while.

I'll eat a head of cabbage every day if it means I'll live a longer and healthier life. But you bet your ass I'm not skipping out on pumpkin pie on Thanksgiving or carrot cake on my birthday. Eat to extend your life, but eat to enjoy your life too. Put that on a fridge magnet.

7. Exfoliate your body, even your lady parts. Your ingrowns will thank you.

There is no greater joy than picking an ingrown hair, but the results of a bikini line picking session are gruesome. Listen to my mom—exfoliate. Not only will it reduce those tempting picking opportunities, but it will keep your skin smoother than a baby's butt. I don't know about you, but I want to feel like a baby's behind forever.

8. Put money aside to get massages. Your body doesn't run like it used to. You're going to need rubdowns.

Just make sure you don't eat too much before you get that massage. Nothing, and I really mean NOTHING, is more terrifying than having to fart while you're getting a massage. You will instantly go from a state of complete relaxation to a place of utter panic in the small amount of time it takes to clench your butt cheeks together.

9. Say no to plans on a Friday because you need a night to yourself.

My introverted ass loves this suggestion but also finds it's imperative. After a week of work, using all my energy to handle everyone else's energy, I am exhausted. If I don't allow myself to take a night off, even on a Friday when you're supposed to be "cool" and go out, I'll start to fall apart. There's nothing cool about being a shell of a human just so you can impress no one by going to a club on a Friday night. Thank god it's Friday and I can stay home to recharge.

10. Say yes to plans on a Saturday because your friends lift your spirits.

My introverted ass hates this suggestion but also knows it's important. Now that I'm older, it takes a lot to moti-vate myself to get up, get dressed, and get out of the house. Especially when I have everything I need at home, or an app to get me whatever I don't. However, there is no app that can replace the power of best friends. A night of laughter, good chats, and unconditional love adds energy to your soul and years to your life. I'm sure of it.

11. Take vitamins daily. Your body is powerful, but why not give it some extra charge?

I take a pile of vitamins every day. Literally, the more letters of the alphabet in pill form I can put in my body, the better. Just do me a favor: If you're going to do the same, consult a doctor on what to take. Instagram models aren't viable resources for vitamin suggestions. They get paid to eat those "hair growth" gummy bears.

12. Get regular facials. It's cheaper than Botox.

The truth is, now that I'm in my thirties, I see my peers panicking to "fix" themselves. I know more people who have had some sort of "work done" than those who haven't. I'm not judging; in fact, I would be lying if I didn't mention I have seriously considered doing the same. I went through a period of time when I sported bangs solely for the purpose of hiding the lines on my forehead. Bangs are ALWAYS a bad idea. My suggestion is if you can set aside money to get facials, your skin will give back by giving you that ageless glow. If you can't swing that, doing your own scrubs and masks will suffice. My mom's face is living proof. Queen looks like a princess.

13. Yoga your stress away, but allow yourself to stay in bed.

My mom has at least one cheesy shirt that says NAMASTAY IN BED on it, but I let it slide because she isn't wrong. Yoga reduces stress, but sometimes the stress of knowing you have to get to yoga to de-stress adds stress. So, wear your cheesy T-shirt in bed all day, and relax the stress away.

14. Wear sunscreen. A tan is cute but avoiding sun damage is cuter.

Plus, there are endless products on the market that can make you look tan without a side of skin cancer. Personally, I stick with the "haven't seen sunlight in a decade" look, but to each their own.

15. Get a pedicure even though you can do it yourself. It gives you time to relax and provides income for someone else.

I am religious about doing this. It's a much-needed scheduled hour for me to do nothing but unwind. I leave my phone in my purse and my mind in the clouds. It also helps maintain my ranking on wikiFeet. This is a dark part of the web that I'm ashamed to be a part of (even though it was not my doing) but proud to have a perfect score on.

16. As you continue to grow and seek new understanding about yourself, journal your feelings and color your thoughts.

I swear it's an effective mental tool, not just a stoner hobby. Although now I can't stop wondering if my mom intended me to smoke weed while I color outside the lines. Whatever you do, don't read your journals while you're stoned. I made the mistake of cracking open a journal, while under the influence, from when I was eight, and I wasted three hours going on an internet dive trying to find the stranger boy who I was convinced was my soul mate because he gave me a slap bracelet at the gas station. There are not enough search terms to find that one kid at the Tarzana Chevron station in the early nineties who slapped his way into my heart.

17. Love the body you're in. You were given it for a reason. Don't let anyone or anything deter you from feeling anything but pride for the skin you're in.

On a more serious note, I began to research plastic surgery during my last relationship because I thought if I fixed my boobs so they were perkier and more even, it would fix my relationship. At the time, we were having serious trouble connecting physically, and it made me insecure to the point of hating my body and the way I looked. Saying that out loud makes me feel so sad. I'm all about doing what you want to do to make yourself feel better, but the idea that I was willing to go under the knife instead of dealing with the real relationship issues is terrifying. Thankfully, I am frightened of all things medical, and researching the process of breast augmentation alone made me feel woozy, so my consideration didn't go any further. No surprise, my relationship ended—it clearly wasn't heading in a healthy direction. After many talks with my therapist, I came to understand that the lack of passion in the relationship was simply a reflection of our dwindling love for each other. It was not, in fact, a result of my boobs, or my body, or anything I could have fixed by a doctor—just a mutual shift in our dynamic that, unexamined, would have cost me a fortune and a foreign addition to my body.

18. Increase your fiber intake. The older you get, the more shit you're holding on to. Literally and figuratively.

I'd also like to suggest investing in a Squatty Potty. They are just as effective as colonics but far less mortifying.

19. Give yourself breast exams because your boobs are important and your life depends on them.

There was an episode of *90210* when Brenda found a lump in her breast, and it freaked me out so much I was afraid to check my own. Ignorance is not bliss, my ladies. That fear was not serving me, but luckily, I came to terms with the importance of doing regular checks, and I've been doing them ever since. Be smart, do your exams, and take care of those perfect boobies. Yes, they are all perfect, even the uneven and less-than-perky ones.

20. Don't sleep in underwear. You need to air out your vagina.

I'm still traumatized by this one. I will not sleep with underwear on. EVER.

*   *   *

I know it's a lot to ask to take time for yourself when you have a whole list of things and people you need to tend to. Even with all my newfound knowledge, it's hard not to feel selfish when turning down plans with friends to spend the night recharging alone, or using some of the money I was going to donate to my goddaughter's school fundraiser for a massage because after I turned thirty I suddenly have back pain. The truth of the matter is that running nonstop on a stress level of ten cripples my mind and body, blocking me from being present or even pleasant to the people around me. Truthfully, getting that massage and taking that night off benefit everyone in my orbit.

And so, last but not least, I'd like to add one suggestion to this list, which I'm certain my mom would agree with.

21. Go on vacations alone.

There is no greater opportunity to focus on your mental and physical health. After all, the most important thing in your life is you. Love yourself, care for you, and no matter what some bozo on a dating app tells you, put yourself first. Self-care is not selfish—it's imperative to your long and gorgeous life.

"You're welcome and thank you," I say as I push the check in your direction. Works every time.

Conclusion

Don't Be Fooled—Everything You See Has a Filter on It

Serenity now!

—Frank Costanza

The life lessons I've picked up over the years are a jumble of contradictions I'm still trying to sort out. Live in the moment, but plan for your future. Face your fears, but please stay safe. Save your money, but life is short. Age is just a number, but your thirty-year-old body says otherwise. With failure comes growth, but don't flunk your STD exam. Relationships take work, but a hard relationship isn't right. Anger is bad, but expressing your emotions is good. Your body is a temple, but French fries are heavenly. Being flawless is boring, but put a filter on your pictures.

How the hell are we supposed to make sense of all this? I so desperately want to do everything right, but trying to walk these fine lines is more challenging than not peeking at my ex-boyfriend's new girlfriend's Instagram account. (Do you think she'll notice if I watch her stories?)

I think it all comes down to doing your best and

accepting that doing things "the right way" is an unattainable goal, even if it appears other people around you are achieving it. How many times have you scrolled through Instagram and felt completely terrible because the people on your feed are not only doing things that appear to be way cooler than what you've got going on, but they also look fucking gorgeous doing it? Have you ever stopped to wonder if they are engaging in these activities specifically for the "gram," or taken into consideration just how many filters and photo-enhancing apps they've run that picture through? I'm not shaming people who work hard to keep up their pristine appearance, but I need to remind myself that the reality of the situation is THIS IS NOT REALITY.

Social media isn't completely to blame, although I do think the accessibility to endless filtered lies certainly doesn't help. I think we've been fed numerous false realities from the minute we were born, and that has encoded us with a drive to seek perfection. Fairy tales, rom-coms, and even comic books (I read one once, so now I'm an expert) instill this idea that happy endings are available and often expected of all of us. Remember what it was like to visit a Disney park, the ultimate utopias when you were a kid (if you were lucky enough to have the opportunity)? It was hard as a kid not to feel a sense of defeat when you left those gates and entered back into the real world. Even as an adult, regardless of the fact that Disneyland is often a chaotic nightmare, I always feel a tinge of sadness leaving the perfectly crafted sweet escape from reality. Why is that? It's probably because Disney has created the kind of perfect world that all of us are striving to achieve. I can tell you firsthand, though, that even Disney uses an insane amount of "filters" to trick you into thinking perfection exists.

That's right—I worked for "The Mouse." I was the stoned, blonde college student who hated every moment inside The Mouse. Literally, INSIDE—I was Mickey Mouse for one long, brutal summer. If you don't see me after this gets published, you can assume the Disney mafia kidnapped me as punishment for telling you that.

I saw, with my own two partially obstructed eyes (thanks to that huge headpiece), all the strict measures Disney goes to in order to trick the guests into thinking everything there is effortlessly flawless. Did you know they pump out fake bakery scents on Main Street so you are enticed to buy all the treats? Not to mention there are countless rules employees have to abide by, like using a very specific "scoop" technique when picking up trash instead of bending over like a normal human. Not sure why seeing someone bend down to grab a wrapper is alarming, but Disney is adamant about hiding it from guests.

I don't mean to crush anyone's dreams by metaphorically taking off the Mickey head. I did that for real once while dressed as Dora the Explorer at a birthday party, and I'm certain I scarred at least two children for life. I blame their mom who insisted I remove my large costume noggin so she could see my face and verify she wasn't

paying for a creep to play with her children. I'll never forget the look of complete terror and confusion as I locked
my real set of eyes with the birthday boy, who broke out
in tears and screams of bloody murder. I'm not sure if he
was more afraid to learn that Dora's head was removable
or that Dora is actually a neurotic Jew who can't speak
Spanish. Either way, I will never make that mistake again.

The point of me telling you all this, besides the fact that
I've been keeping my Mickey Mouse identity a secret for
years and needed to get it off my chest, is that I had an eye-
opening experience at Disney that granted me the understanding that filtered perfection is a dangerous enemy to
the ego and unless I identify these people, places, and
things as fabricated versions of themselves, I will crumble
in self-doubt and unjustified judgment.

This all happened two years ago, ironically not when I
was working at Disneyland, but when I brought my then-
serious boyfriend of one year with me to visit my godbabies in Orlando for Christmas. This was a terrible idea
for several reasons: (1) I don't think I believe in God. (2) I
definitely don't believe in Orlando. (3) A trip to Florida is
anything but romantic.

Welcome to Orlando, Florida—nicknamed "The City
Beautiful." Not only is this name grammatically incorrect,
which is a delightful reflection of the general population's
IQ, but also the city is far from beautiful. It is full of crazy
drivers, endless strip malls, slow-moving tourists, and terrible fashion sensibilities. I'm no style guru, but I can confidently say cargo shorts and socks with sandals are not on

trend. I only visit the place because Laurel, my dear friend and former business partner, lives there with my three gorgeous godbabies. Can you believe she trusted me to be a godmom? Like, I legitimately signed a document that stated should she and her husband both die, I would have full custody of these three children. I have never wanted someone to not die more than I do them. Don't get me wrong, these kids are fantastic, but the thought of inheriting three kids overnight is a nightmare. Not only would I be a single mom of three with no experience or qualifications for such a role, but I would also most likely have to move to Orlando.

I thought it would be nice to take a trip with my boyfriend at the time. Our relationship was getting serious, and I wanted him to meet his future children, should there be a double death—that's not what I told him, but I think it was implied. I also love any excuse to stay in a hotel, especially with a significant other. Something about a hotel makes sex so much better. I'd like to think it's the romance sparked by being in a new city with no real responsibilities, but really the main appeal is being able to mess up the sheets without having to wash them after. The amount of strength and effort it takes to put on the fitted sheet that has been dried a few too many times is extreme. I've pulled several muscles over the years doing just that. So, I will always find joy in flipping the sign to MAKE UP ROOM after a vacation romp.

Laurel and her family moved to a small part of town called Celebration. Let it be known they are fully aware of how bizarre the town is and consider themselves to be fish out of filtered water. Seriously, if you haven't heard of Celebration, Florida, you have to look it up—it's unreal, an actual facade. It's a "master planned community" developed by the Walt Disney Company, where, just like the theme parks, everything is pristine. The downtown consists of one main street with one Chinese restaurant, one Japanese restaurant, one Greek restaurant, one Mexican restaurant, one American restaurant, and a Starbucks. The small community is filled with affluent families with large, gas-guzzling "mommy vans" branded with religious bumper stickers and I BRAKE FOR MICKEY MOUSE license plate frames. The neighborhood is framed by perfectly groomed landscaping and rustic bridges and bike paths that trick you into believing they were always there and not dug up out of a swamp in the early nineties.

At first, Celebration was beyond charming—it felt like we were on a movie set, or hanging out in *Leave It to Beaver*. We rode bikes, walked around the lake, shopped in the local trinket shops. After spending some time there, I began feeling a sense of insecurity about the less-than-ideal town I was living in, without any children or a gorgeous ring on my finger. Laurel and her family, in this town, were akin to a glossy picture you'd see in a magazine. It was hard not to be jealous.

As the trip went on, though, the facade of everything in front of me began to deteriorate. Starting with the town itself, which, according to Laurel, was falling apart. Apparently, some of the condos in Celebration that look picturesque from the outside were actually crumbling on the inside. Her guess was they were built in a hurry and with cheap material. Whatever the case, roofs were leaking, mold was spreading, and balconies were starting to collapse. The townspeople were dealing with lawsuits and daily fights with the local reps—not exactly the Pleasantville they had bought into.

We planned to spend a day with Laurel and the kids at Disney World, because that is the only thing to do in Orlando besides shoot your guns and go to a buffet. In preparation for the day, we helped Laurel pack up her smashed-Cheerio-covered van. It wasn't until the third trip back to the trunk that I realized I had never really taken into account the amount of shit it requires to take kids anywhere. I always see pictures of my friends and their kids, packed in their cars, smiling and looking like they are having the best time. What I never was privy to was the solid thirty-minute load-in—and that was with the assistance of two additional adults. Once we were all in, and some shitty kids' song was playing on repeat, we headed to the park. In the short amount of time it took to get there, there were three meltdowns, two snack breaks, and one poop. I was already tired and it wasn't even 10 a.m. God bless parents—that is not a job for the weak. When we finally got into the park, I was hit with a wave of anxiety. Maybe it was the insane amount of people, the intense Florida sun even in winter, or some PTSD from my summer working for The Mouse, but I knew this wasn't going to be easy.

I wasn't wrong. The next few hours consisted of one long line after another, on-again-off-again kid tantrums, and constant swiping of my credit card because I couldn't help but buy those little boogers the useless shit Disney had ingeniously placed at their eye level. Disney also appears to do a great job of somehow making you believe spending doesn't count when you're there. It seemed like everyone in the park was sporting copious amounts of bullshit merchandise, without a care.

I don't mean to sound like a party pooper; it's just that I had a growing awareness of the insincerity all around me that I couldn't shake. Not to mention I was lugging around several pounds of shit inside of me because you can't find a vegetable to save your life at Disney. Does Mickey not believe in fiber?

My boyfriend didn't seem to be bothered by any of the Disney World nonsense; he was having a genuinely fantastic time with the kids. Carrying them on his shoulders, playing games with them while we waited in lines, holding their hands on the scary rides. To an outsider looking in, he was doing everything right, everything a girlfriend could want. Yet, I started to feel myself pull away from him, noticing I wasn't eager to hold his hand or be by his side like I usually was. I found myself nitpicking everything he was saying, internally judging and noting all the things that I thought were annoying about him. At the time, I couldn't pinpoint why I was doing this; instead I just shoved the feelings way, way down and went on with the day. Little did I realize all my emotions would soon come back up. Literally.

The good thing about hanging out with kids, besides eating snacks you otherwise would never buy (I'm a grown-ass woman watching her weight; I cannot justify buying Fruit by the Foot anymore, but you better believe I love stealing me some three feet of flattened artificial nonsense from a three-year-old), is that they don't last very long doing anything. By 5 p.m., we were long gone from the Land of Simulated Joy and Empty Wallets, but just when I thought we were in the clear of kid-related activities, I was let in on the fact that you're NEVER done with kid-related *anything*. With the end of one extravagant event comes another, because the only way to keep children from having meltdowns is to present them with fake snowfall two times a night for the entire month of December. No joke—this is what they do in Celebration, Florida.

We sat on the patio of the Chinese restaurant as the kids made snow angels in the suds that shot out from the vents above Main Street. Christmas music played, laughter filled the air, a horse-drawn carriage circled the block, and my boyfriend whispered in my ear, "I want to be with you forever." It was one of those perfect moments you see in the movies, you read about in romance novels, you dream about one day experiencing, but still it didn't feel right to me. Everything seemed incredibly crafted and completely inauthentic, including his grand declaration, and all I could do was smile back with glossed-over eyes.

Feeling guilty that I was so disconnected, I looked around to try to find something genuine and real to help ground me. As soon as I did, I began to notice even more holes in this "perfect" moment.

First, it seemed like everyone in town was white. I darted my eyes around, desperately searching for some diversity. Coming from Los Angeles, where we are blessed with a melting pot of cultures, this is a very unsettling feeling. It's not that it was unacceptable to be another race in Celebration—in fact, everyone was so absurdly kind there; I'm assuming they would fake acceptance regardless of their true feelings. Which, if you've seen *Get Out*, is potentially even scarier. Hoping that wasn't the case, it still gave me chills realizing the kids in the town would know nothing different. I started to feel a little claustrophobic, as if I had just discovered I was actually in a bubble, because I was.

I continued my quest for normalcy, when it came to my attention that there were no homeless people. Again, another culture shock coming from a town that is sadly overpopulated with people living on the streets. How could this be? Was this a city mandate? Do they bus the homeless elsewhere? If I were without a home, this perfect, safe town would be the first place I'd try to stay. There must be a plan implemented to keep them out. That's heartbreaking. I started to feel my chest getting heavy.

I kept searching for something grounding, at this point completely disengaged with the dinner conversation or my boyfriend. The more I looked, the worse it got. There were no trashcans in town. No billboards. No individuality.

Everything was in perfect order. Everything looked the same. Families arrived to the main street in droves. Each car bigger than the next. Every family with at least three kids, completely disregarding any concern for overpopulation. Everyone was taking pictures, over and over again, selfie sticks raised, hoping to get the perfect shot to put on their perfect social media accounts, to show off their perfect life.

I looked across the table at my boyfriend, who now appeared as just another character enjoying being a part of this weird world. Did he not see what I was seeing? Did this not all freak him out too? Did he want to get married, have a million babies, and pretend like we were happy? Am I even happy? My temples began to throb. My brain was overwhelmed, trying to process the concept of family and babies and Mickey and consumerism and Christmas and happiness and...I...COULDN'T...BREATHE. Another breakdown for the books. (Pun not intended but I did just give myself a high five.)

Maybe it was the MSG or my poor digestion of the town, but I ended up throwing up all night. For some reason, we had a hotel room with two beds (which I think was ultimately foreshadowing the story of our relationship). My boyfriend was passed out in one bed, so when I finally stopped vomiting, I laid down alone in the other one. I stared at the ceiling, tears streaming down my face, running every question through my brain.

"I'm thirty-three years old. What the fuck am I doing? What the fuck do I want? Who the fuck am I? What the fuck is MSG?" I leaned over and threw up one more time, straight onto the floor, missing the trashcan completely. That was my trip to Disney World. Not exactly Instagram worthy.

There is a happy ending to this tale, although not your traditional one. This is the honest conclusion, which started with me visiting my therapist many times to figure out why I was so deeply affected by that trip. I knew it wasn't Celebration or Disney World that was the problem. It was the pressure I felt when I saw Laurel and her gorgeous family in that seemingly perfect little town. It was me comparing myself to my surroundings from the minute we got there, making me insecure to the point of convincing myself that my boyfriend was more attracted to Laurel than to me. He did NOTHING to indicate this—I was just so wrapped up in my head that I began thinking nonsense.

It wasn't until I started to see the cracks in the presentations around me that it clicked—I was trying to measure up to something that would never be achievable, because it didn't exist in the first place. It was all fabricated. With that realization, I started wondering what else was being faked in my life, specifically questioning if I had been convincing myself I was in love with my boyfriend because I wanted to have the "ideal relationship" so badly. Sadly, the answer was yes; I was in a relationship that wasn't wholly right for me, because I wanted so badly to have my happy ever after. Upon realizing I had been ignoring my true feelings—and it wasn't healthy for either of us—we decided to break up and go our separate ways. Even though it hurt deeply, and I wish I could have done it sooner, I was proud of myself for ultimately listening to my heart and making a choice that combatted the innate fear of being alone. Taking this more pragmatic approach helped speed the healing process along. That and hibernating with my dog and takeout for a few weeks.

After some time, I got back into the dating app saddle just to test the waters and see what it felt like. I'll tell you what, dating at this age is actually the best. I know what I want, who I want, and I'm not afraid to wait until I find what I'm looking for. I casually combed through the options, not taking the task too seriously. I hardly swiped right, because I can sniff out the bullshit now, and I just don't have the energy to fuck around. When I finally saw a guy that appeared genuine and seemed to fit my ideal wish list perfectly, I swiped right to happily find he had too. We chatted like we had known each other for years, so I mustered up the courage to say yes and go on a date with him. Within seconds of meeting, I knew this was the person I'm actually supposed to be with now, without expectations of where it will lead or what our future holds. Just here, in the now, and it's been awesome ever since.

Today I turned thirty-five. I thought I would be panicked when I woke up. I figured this would be the apex of my thirty-life crisis. I also thought I'd find new lines on my face and my tits would be an inch closer to my toes, but I don't feel or see any of that. I mean, I did get an intense antiaging facial last night and I'm wearing a fantastic bra, but still, no breakdown. In fact, I feel great. Maybe it took the last four years of pure anxiety to get to this point, but in this moment, I feel confident and hopeful that moving forward I will be able to move through my life with the understanding that I'm writing my own story, not trying to follow along with some popular romance flick.

I am thirty-five. I am not married, I don't have kids, I support myself, my pants are a little tight, and I've never been happier.

I didn't share my thirty-life crisis with you in order to show off how much progress I've made. I'm not even going to begin to claim that this happiness won't subside at points, my anxiety won't creep back in, or I'll never throw a filter on a picture that I think I look old in. I simply wanted to offer a look into the life of someone who was caught off guard by the perils that came with turning thirty in the hope that there is at least one takeaway for you. If nothing else, hopefully you had a good laugh at all my crazy mishaps and embarrassing mistakes. If you got this far, I'm proud of your reading skills. I'm also honored that you went on this journey with me.

Go kick some ass in your life. Surround yourself with people who accept you for you and puppies who lick you when you're down. Go to therapy, create your boundaries, say no to gender-reveal parties. Replace judgment with curiosity, ask for help, set your Tinder standards high, wear your favorite overalls, leave the filters off, watch reruns of *Seinfeld*. Have your heart broken, eat French fries, and open your heart back up. Feel free to reread this book and buy a ton of copies for all your friends, referring to me as Blonde Oprah. Live your life with kindness and joy, compassion and honesty. Most importantly, try to remember that you are absolutely enough.

Until my forty-life crisis, friends.

Epilogue

A Year Later

*What is this obsession people have with books? They
put them in their houses—like they're trophies.
What do you need it for after you read it?*

—Jerry Seinfeld

A year has gone by since I wrote this book, and now, the
thirty-six-year-old version of me is stunned at the amount
of changes I have endured since I first started writing. It's
bizarre to think we know ourselves so well, but when we
have access to a porthole into our old thoughts and former
selves, we are swiftly reminded of just how much we can
grow in a short amount of time.

Just last year I was convinced I wasn't destined for a
wedding or kids, and I rebelled with booze and casual
dating. Three hundred and sixty-five-plus days later, I am
Googling wedding rings and even having moments when
I think having a baby would be kind of awesome, exploding poops and all. What the actual fuck? Who am I? How
did this happen? And what in the world will next year
look like at this rate?

Epilogue

At the end of the last chapter, I mentioned pushing myself to get "back in the game" by going on a date. I was reluctant to go, knowing I wasn't 100 percent ready to jump back into the dating world, but I figured I had to throw myself into the fire at some point to be reminded that I was still capable of such a daunting task. Also, you know your girl loves a free drink, so at least I had that tangible and delicious incentive.

I remember how nervous I was on my Uber ride over to the bar. I hadn't been on a date since my breakup, so the feeling of panic was beginning to flood my body. Lucky for me, I had a chatty driver who was going on and on about her ex who she was convinced was cheating on her with some dude, distracting me from going down my usual full-blown preworry spiral. I didn't bother to tell her about my past with a gay boyfriend—I figured that would just rile her up to the point of unsafe driving—so instead I just enjoyed the distraction while I nervously patted down my sweaty armpits in the backseat.

When I got out and started walking toward the bar, I saw him heading toward me. Jeff from Bumble, just like his pictures. Smile radiant, eyes bright, body slamming, and outfit—totally terrible. Don't judge a date by their nineties vest and oversize leather jacket. Lucky for me, and him, the minute we started talking everything clicked into place and the horror of his dated fashion choices faded away. He was inquisitive, grounded, hilarious, genuine, and mature. Our conversations flowed effortlessly, and our chemistry was palpable. He could have been wearing a dress at that point and I'd still want to make out with him. Which we did end up doing, back at my house, as I cleverly slipped his vest off, making the almost perfect match before me flawless. That was the start of what has been the greatest love I've ever known.

Call it fate, luck, or so many shitty dating experiences that I deserve a break, but it turns out I finally met my person. Not the person I forced myself into being attracted to because on paper he was ideal, or the one I desperately tried to convince to love me regardless of his clear resistance, but the man who effortlessly waltzed into my life when I wasn't really ready and completed the puzzle I had been trying to solve all these years. Dude, I know—it sounds like a fucking cliché, but it seriously happened when I wasn't looking for it.

I'm now sharing my home, my dog, and my bed with this man. The bed part, by the way, is totally bonkers when I really break it down. For thirty-five years, minus the few when I lived with Shane, I had my own bed, a very personal and singular thing. It didn't occur to me, until last night, when Jeff and I rolled over and started laughing, that I now share a bed—as in I will never have my own again. It seems so obvious and immaterial, but it's a reality I couldn't have imagined accepting, even just a year ago. "Mine" has turned to "ours," "me" has turned to "we," and "I" have turned into "a total mush who is completely in love and barely recognizes herself."

This is not all to say that finding a partner is the ultimate end goal and the answer to happiness; trust me—being in a relationship, no matter how wonderful it is, is still a ton of work. (Where's the guide on how to be an independent skeptic of love in a healthy partnership?) Rather, I mention this all as a reminder that we are sent on paths we could never plan for regardless of how much we worry or try to manage every moment along the way. Sorry, control freaks—you got to sit this one out.

It seems to me that every year brings more wisdom and a clearer sense of self, which is a decent trade-off for the inevitable increase in wrinkles and gray hairs. For example, throughout my twenties and up until this last year, I wore hair extensions fairly consistently. I know it sounds rather ridiculous that this could result in a life-altering experience, but hear me out. For me, my extensions were a direct (and expensive) reflection of the insecurities I carried around with me all these years. I had never been 100 percent confident in who I was or how I looked, so I controlled what I could by adding pounds of real hair, from god knows where, in order to fabricate confidence. You know that pesky pocket of fat that lives between your armpit and your arm that's impossible to get rid of? You can't see those fuckers if you have long hair to cover them up. Want to look like most of the twenty-year-olds you see on Instagram these days? Get yourself some lengthy locks, and you magically look five years younger.

The extensions worked, at least on a surface level, but like any Band-Aid they only covered the problem, never actually healing it. Even though I had been actively working on gaining self-love and acceptance, it wasn't until earlier this year that I actually started to love my body as is, finding my age to be empowering rather than embarrassing, and feeling secure enough to let the extensions go. I mean, let's be real—I still dye my hair and I'm not convinced I'll never put the fake ones back in, but in this moment, I finally love the real(-ish) me. Maybe confidence and acceptance are granted with time. Or maybe we just continue to grow, discover, and love ourselves at our own pace regardless of our age.

I have a very distinct memory of watching *The Real World* in high school and thinking everyone in the house was so much older and far cooler than me. I wanted so badly to look and act like them; I even thought it would be "super rad" to be on the show one day. Then around the time I graduated from college, I remember tuning back in and realizing just how young and totally dumb these cast members were for signing up to do that. Maybe that's not the fairest assessment—I was surely the less-than-bright one who watched every season of the damn show. I just bring this up not only to admit that I still watch every crappy MTV reality show, but also to give an example of the frequently changing perspective that comes with every year. In a blink of an eye, something that seems so out of reach can become attainable or even an unwanted thing of the past.

Obviously, there are far more important subject matters that parallel this embarrassing *Real World* example, like marriage and babies, but I've talked so much about those topics I'm exhausted thinking about them. I've just decided that, moving forward, I'm going to take things one day at a time and see where the wind takes me. Perhaps in a year I'll have a ring on my finger, or a baby in my belly, but if not, I'm sure there's something else coming that I could have never planned for. I think it's safe to say "Never say never" is some legit advice, because regardless of what you think and expect to happen, you can never properly anticipate what's right around the corner. Except for being cast on *The Real World*—I can confidently say I will NEVER be on the show. (My high school heart is slightly broken.)

For now, I'll put this book and these chapters of my life on the shelf and move forward with grace and zest. But when I feel lost or unsure of my abilities to get through a tough situation, I'll take it back out and remind myself that I did it before, I can do it again, and I will always come out better for it.

Getting old doesn't suck; it's actually kind of awesome. I just need to be reminded of that, time and again, when the aches and pains and the elongated hangovers kick in. There's nothing a long bath, a juicy docuseries, and an overpoured glass of wine for dinner can't fix. You're an adult now. You have every right to indulge and enjoy it.

Can't wait to see what's next. Cheers, old farts. You're fantastic.

Acknowledgments

I'm speechless. I have no speech!
—George Costanza

I used to practice Oscar acceptance speeches in the shower, not book acknowledgments—I'm unprepared! Besides, an acknowledgment doesn't even begin to express the gratitude I feel toward everyone who has inspired me and held my hand through this process. Thank you to all the wonderful people who watch me on YouTube; it's because of you I get to do insane things like write a book. I can only hope I have more opportunities to continue to entertain you across many platforms. Thank you to my managers, Jason Newman and Kendall Rhodes, who have believed in me way before they had proper reason to. Kirby Kim and the team at Janklow & Nesbit, I'm beyond grateful for your unwavering confidence in this weirdo from the internet. I'm forever indebted to Suzanne O'Neill and Grand Central Publishing for your guidance and your willingness to take a chance on a new writer in overalls. Sarah Branham, my editor and cheerleader, thank you for your endless wisdom, inquiries, and grammar help. Aron Giannini and my team over at Abrams, I can't thank you enough, or wonder why you guys are so good to me. My lawyer, Danny Miller, you are a gentleman, a friend, and a protective badass. Shane Dawson, you changed my life—no amount of thanks will suffice. To my friends, some mentioned, others (who are probably relieved) not, YOU are the reason I am who I am. I have extracted little bits and pieces from you all, in the least creepy way possible, and I cannot thank you enough. To my godbabies and favorite tiny ones: Lily, Ella, Milo, Harrison, Levi, and June, thank you for showing me what undeniable love feels like and providing me with an excuse to never have kids of my own. Thank you to my therapist, who will never be able to tell anyone her client wrote about her. To Corny, my dog who can read. To all my teachers along the way—you never get enough credit or compensation. To past boyfriends and terrible dates, who have given me endless material and lessons that I hold near and dear. To Jeff, thanks for that one joke and those two words, and for loving me even after you read this…hopefully. You are my heart and my world. To my family: Dad, Mom, Adam, Coree, Grandma, Grandpa, and the rest of the gang, I am humbled by your hearts, minds, and spirits. You make me proud to be a Schwartz. Thank you for loving me, accepting me, and encouraging me, even when I was a real shit-head. I love you unconditionally. To the overthinkers, the worrywarts, the weirdos, the untraditional path takers, and the introverts, I get you. I am you. And I'm here to remind you you're doing great. Lastly, Larry David and Jerry Seinfeld, you thought you were writing a show about nothing. In reality, you were writing the script to my life. So, thank you, I think.

About the Author

Lisa is an actress, writer, and producer born in Los Angeles, and raised on *Seinfeld*. She is best known for her YouTube channel, Lisbug, which features original comedic and musical content. To date, Lisa has garnered more than 2.2 million unique subscribers. Her most popular video, a parody of Taylor Swift's "Shake It Off," generated 20 million views and received coverage in several outlets, including the *Huffington Post*. Lisa also co-created and starred in *Party Girl*, an original scripted series for Freeform, as well as *This Isn't Working* for ABC Digital. She has hosted various digital segments for ABC's *The Bachelor, Seventeen*, and Yahoo. She can be heard as the voice of Talking Angela in the *Talking Tom and Friends* show on Netflix and Rube in the animated feature film *The Ladybug. Thirty-Life Crisis* is Lisa's first book, but not her first crisis.